"Once I finished *5 M*... ...d it again; it was such a breath of fresh ... ... .te the significance and severity of my personal stresses in relation to the big picture and forever changed my perspective. I was reminded that in the grand scheme of life, the worries that weigh me down are extremely insignificant and that realization alone provides relief! This is a perfect book to have on your desk at the office for quick encouragement and practical tips when you feel the stress knocking on your door."

—Cindy Maguire, account director,
Leo Burnett Advertising, Chicago

"WOW…*5 Minutes to Stress Relief* has some real 'eye openers.' While prompting us to really think about what is important in this lifetime, it also provides guidance on how to appreciate everything we are. Examples were easy to relate to and the valuable message(s) are applicable to both men and women, whether you're part of the "corporate world" or not."

—Barbara Erbacher, senior executive assistant,
Ball Aerospace & Technologies Corp.

"As an opera singer whose work has included jazz, Broadway and modern music performances, coping with the mega stress associated with living and auditioning in NYC is a daily struggle. Lauren is my stress relief guru. Many of the quick techniques she teaches and shares in *5 Minutes to Stress Relief* eliminate fear and self-doubt which has led to some of the best performances of my life! EFT is crazy simple and it works on the spot. Since I started applying the techniques Lauren taught me I have been engaged and offered a re-engagement with Opéra de Toulon in Southern France, Sportin' Life in Gershwin's Porgy and Bess with the Virginia Opera, concert appearances with the Buck Hill-Skytop Music Festival, and an invitation to appear in the NYC 75th Anniversary Concert to honor Porgy and Bess all in one year! Thank you Lauren for reminding me that ALL things are possible even doing life without stressing out!"

—Lawrence Craig, Opera Singer/Actor

"My life is full of constant demands and pressures, on the work front as managing partner of a PR firm and as a mother of three young kids. I have very little time to myself so carving out stress-free moments in my day is critical. I utilize Lauren's stress relieving techniques found in *5 Minutes to Stress Relief* daily to reduce the anxiety in my life. It helps me work through problems and find resolution, which in turn lowers my stress. For example, during the 2010 mid-term elections I worked with the media for Colorado's United States Senate race—the most heated race in the country."

—Amy Jewett, CEO Real PR

"As an actor and standup comic living in NYC, mega stress is a daily struggle. Fear of being judged and not getting a laugh or certain acting part can be overwhelming. I have literally called Lauren from the bathroom before a big performance and asked this stress relief goddess to help me believe in myself again and stop stressing myself out! She has given me quick and easy techniques to overcome my fears and has helped me give the best performances of my life— ironically by letting go. Since she taught me EFT, which is a technique found in *5 Minutes to Stress Relief,* I have booked two national spots on ABC's *What Would You Do?* (Featured on Good Morning America) a gig at Caroline's on Broadway, and a national commercial all in one year! I can't thank her enough!"

—Carla Johnston, screen writer/actress

"I've travelled the world documenting individuals who have overcome physical and emotional issues using faith, prayer, and energy medicine. Lauren is not only a survivor, but she has the gift of knowing what others will experience on their own healing journeys and how to support them. Her insights found in *5 Minutes to Stress Relief* along with her advice and compassion are beautiful to witness and are a standout in the work I am doing to profile individuals like her. Lauren Miller is destined to become a champion for the power of energy medicine to help us all find our own ability to heal. If one needs an answer to why certain people are challenged with devastating illnesses or events in their lives, Lauren provides one very obvious and joyous answer—she offers us a model for hope."

—Eric Hurre, documentary film producer

5 Minutes to Stress Relief

How to Release Fear, Worry, and Doubt...*Instantly*

By Lauren E. Miller

Foreword by Les Brown

The Career Press, Inc.
Pompton Plains, NJ

5 MINUTES TO STRESS RELIEF
EDITED AND TYPESET BY GINA TALUCCI
Cover design by Joanna Williams Designs
Printed in the U.S.A.

To order this title, please call toll-free 1-800-CAREER-1 (NJ and Canada: 201-848-0310) to order using VISA or MasterCard, or for further information on books from Career Press.

CAREER
PRESS

The Career Press, Inc.
220 West Parkway, Unit 12
Pompton Plains, NJ 07444
www.careerpress.com

Library of Congress Cataloging-in-Publication Data
Miller, Lauren E.
  5 minutes to stress relief : how to release worry, fear, and
  doubt...instantly / by Lauren E. Miller.
          p. cm.
Includes index.
ISBN 978-1-60163-256-2 -- ISBN 978-1-60163-537-2 (ebook)
1. Stress (Psychology)--Religious aspects--Christianity. I. Title.
II. Title: Five minutes to stress relief.
      BV4908.5.M55 2013
      155.9'042--dc23
                                        2012047114

Dedication

To my beautiful friend Juney June, who chose to play the infinite game of life versus the finite game, who knew what was essential and non-essential.

Sweet Juney, you laughed and sang on earth all the way up to the moment your heart stopped beating on earth and began to beat in the heavenly realms. Thank you for teaching me how to move through fear back to God again and again and again. For reminding me that God has given me the ability to laugh, love, and sing no matter what surrounds me. I will carry the strength of your positive perspectives within my heart and out into the world... until we meet face to face once again.

Acknowledgments

With profound gratitude, I would like to thank my "A" team:

God, for the grace at each new dawn, to choose life and love, no matter what surrounds me.

My precious husband, Dean, and our three children, Kaylin, Jay, and Kimberly, for all of the laughter, love, and joy you bring into my life.

My mom and dad, for seeing me for who I am and loving all they see.

My sister, Kimberly, who continued to show up for me in the eye of the storm, sometimes in the middle of the night, even though she lives several states away.

My close friends and family, who hold my hand and cheer me on, reminding me of my God-given ability to create beauty, walk on water, and move mountains.

Joanne Shwed (*www.authoronestop.com*), a highly talented editor, who has the amazing gift of organizing expansive, creative thoughts.

Randy Peyser (*www.authoronestop.com*), an incredibly gifted book consultant, who saw this entire project through to completion.

John Willig (*www.literaryservicesinc.com*), my agent, for seeing the impact that one person, who hears the voice of inner inspiration and acts on it, can have in the world.

The tribe of beautiful people gathered at Career Press/New Page Books, who caught the wind of creative motivation and inspiration blowing through my life and allowed it to move through the world for a greater good.

Medical Disclaimer

Any information found within *5 Minutes to Stress Relief* is for general educational and informational purposes only. Such information is not intended or otherwise implied to be medical advice. Understand that such information is by no means complete or exhaustive and that, as a result, such information does not encompass all conditions, disorders, health-related issues, or respective treatments.

You should always consult your physician or health care provider to determine the appropriateness of this information for your own situation, medical condition, or treatment plan.

Any information contained in *5 Minutes to Stress Relief*, including, but not limited to, product descriptions and customer testimonials, should not be used for the diagnosis and treatment of any health issue or for the prescription of any medication or treatment.

Contents

Foreword

Because of unemployment, foreclosures, and the volatile economic times in which we live, more people are feeling overwhelmed, hopeless, and stressed out. *5 Minutes to Stress Relief* provides you with tried and proven methods that will give you the mindset and key strategies that will anchor your mind, calm your spirit, and connect you with your higher self. Lauren Miller—author, dynamic speaker, media stress expert, and seminar facilitator—shares her life-saving techniques that will give you the mental, emotional, and spiritual resiliency to handle everything that life throws at you.

During my second and final battle with cancer, Lauren taught me the value of living my life from a place of power by surrendering and releasing. Studies show that stress is wreaking havoc on our relationships and on our jobs, and most importantly robbing us from our health and peace of mind.

This book is full of stress-relieving strategies that you can use in your daily life at home, in traffic, on the job, or on the run. Lauren Miller's methods work if you work it. She is a master at teaching you how to keep stress in check.

—Les Brown
Mrs. Mamie Brown's Baby Boy
Author, speaker, and speech coach
God Bless the Day You Were Born

Preface

Throughout the years I've learned firsthand as I walked through two of life's top stressors at the same time, advanced cancer and divorce, that my choice of focus makes all the difference in the outcome. As you read through these pages, the power contained in your choice of focus and desired outcomes will easily expand. Stress is simply a signal within the body offering the opportunity to identify and adjust your perception of any situation. It is my belief that the three main fuels of stress are: fear, worry, and doubt.

I am confident that my conscious choice to choose God, life, and love over fear, worry, and doubt, along with what the white coats told me, played a major role in my complete healing and restoration.

Going through the experience of losing any familiar recognition of my physical appearance as I lost my hair and breasts during the two years of treatment offered me an expansive opportunity to embrace the source of my true identity. My son, who was 10 years old at the time of the cancer diagnosis, reminded me of this opportunity when he saw me weeping over the loss of my hair as he said, "Mom, don't cry. Your soul still has hair." One small piece of essential information resulted in a complete shift in perspective.

I believe that one of the greatest positions of empowerment lies in your conscious choice to stay awake at the gate of your thoughts. A thought is an objective observation of life taken in through your five senses until you label it as a threat. As soon as you label the thought as threatening to your safety (spiritually, emotionally, or physically) stress seeps in and begins to have its way within your body. Your body listens very closely to what you think down to the cellular level, and you will learn more about the depth of this reality within the pages of this book.

It is my intention for the insights contained within these pages that you, the reader, emerge knowing specific stress relief skills, perceptions, and techniques that you can apply immediately to your life to expand your faith, sense of purpose, inner calm, clear focus, motivation, and solution-based thinking.

Knowing that stress walks hand in hand with disease, I am dedicated to continual education and practice in the areas of stress and anxiety relief. I often feel that I am still wearing this *earth suit* for the sole purpose of guiding people back to their fullest God-given natural state of being: faith-filled, joyful, peaceful, and creative and love-infused. May it be the case for you as you read through the book.

"Dear God increase my love for your people so that my priorities align with my divinity."

Introduction:
Don't Stress Out When You Read
This Stress Relief Manual!

The goal of this book is to create a "stress-free" stress relief manual, which I have designed in a simple, easy-to-understand format. This book will provide optimal "Grab-and-Go" moments to guide individuals and entire corporations into the experience of stress-free living on the job and in life.

The information in this book honors the uniqueness of every human being. Take what works for you to create your own stress relief program. After all, no one knows better than you do what gives you a sense of empowerment and inner peace. Be present to what inspires you as you read. Take what you connect with—your "a-ha" moment—and act on it.

Try one or two different techniques every couple of days, such as a spontaneous movement moment (Chapter 13) in an elevator, or erase and replace (Chapter 8).

People gravitate toward that which is familiar to them in life. If you are used to the energy of victimization, which manifests in complaining and focusing on what is *not* working out, that's where you will hang out. When you choose to move into the "unfamiliar," which might include shifting your focus to what *is* working out for you and taking full responsibility for your life, be patient with yourself and the process. It takes time and commitment to make the shift, so perhaps start with a month of daily practice on the techniques that work for you and go from there.

An abundance of different stress relief techniques and practices are included in this book. Each has proven success, and you can do many of them in less than five minutes to release stress. I present each technique and practice with simple explanations so the reader can start applying them today. Remember: Be creative and playful. Humor has a direct effect on our cellular function and overall health, so don't take these exercises too seriously when trying them for the first time.

To your peace and joy,
Lauren E. Miller

1

How Do You Manifest Your Stress?

Do any of the following statements sound familiar? According to the American Psychological Association:

~ *Three-quarters of Americans experience symptoms related to stress in a given month, including:*

   ~ *77% who experience physical symptoms.*

   ~ *73% who experience psychological symptoms.*

~ *One-third of Americans feel they are living with extreme stress.*

~ *About one-half of Americans (48%) feel that their stress has increased in the past five years.*

~ *Money and work are the leading causes of stress (mentioned by 75% of Americans).*

~ *Physical symptoms of stress include:*
  ~ *Fatigue (51%).*
  ~ *Headache (44%).*
  ~ *Upset stomach (34%).*
  ~ *Muscle tension (30%).*
  ~ *Change in appetite (23%).*
  ~ *Teeth grinding (17%).*
  ~ *Change in sex drive (15%).*
  ~ *Dizziness (13%).*

~ *Psychological symptoms of stress include:*
  ~ *Irritability or anger (50%).*
  ~ *Nervousness (45%).*
  ~ *Lack of energy (45%).*
  ~ *Feeling as though you could cry (35%).*

~ *Stress impacts lives in dramatic ways:*
  ~ *About one-half of Americans say that stress has a negative impact on both their personal and professional lives.*
  ~ *About one-third (31%) of employed adults have difficulty managing work and family responsibilities.*
  ~ *More than one-third (35%) of employed adults cite jobs interfering with their family or personal time as a significant source of stress.*
  ~ *Stress causes more than half of Americans (54%) to fight with people close to them.*

~ *One in four people report that they have been alienated from a friend or family member because of stress.*

~ *8% of Americans connect stress to divorce or separation.*[1]

~ *Workplace stress costs more than $300 billion each year in healthcare, missed work, and stress reduction.*[2]

~ *Workers who report that they are stressed incur healthcare costs that are 46% higher, or an average of $600 more per person, than non-stressed employees.*[3]

Corporate stress is one of the most common forms of stress in our society. Public speaking, job security, lateral communication, absenteeism, meetings, time crunch/deadlines, performance reviews, quotas, budgets, and phobias of crowds, closed spaces (elevators), and flying are among the top triggers of corporate stress.

Take action

Stress is simply a signal within your body that gives you the opportunity to identify and adjust your perception of any situation. You are not a victim to life unless you choose to be, and many people who suffer from workplace stress fall into that category.

Practice being the observer of your life instead of the reactor. Practice becoming a curious human being about everything that unfolds before you. When you play the part of watcher, you begin to remember that you have time to consider how you want to respond. Because we live in such a fast-paced society, we often fall victim to time. Carve out moments between what happens before you and your desired response to it. Practice slowing time down. By thinking before you react, you choose how you want to form your life.

Perhaps you have an old pattern of thinking that says, "I need to move quickly and respond instantly in order to achieve or reach my goals." However, if you created that program, you are in a position to change it to fit the kind of life you desire to create.

Ask yourself, "Am I living at a pace of life that lends itself to moments of inner peace?" If the answer is no, I invite you to reconsider the price you may pay with regard to your physical well-being. As Proverbs 13:30 says so brilliantly: "A heart at peace gives *life* to the body."

I am speaking from personal experience. As a Type A personality I burned the candle at both ends, and my body could not keep up. Because I did not take the time to align myself spiritually, emotionally, and physically, the random cancer cells had their way with me.

Infuse your days with moments of stillness. Throughout history, mankind has been able to encounter peace in the presence of stillness. This book will show you how to take back your ability to slow down time and realign yourself with what you value most.

2

What's Really Going on Behind All of the Stress?

What would you dare to do in life if you knew you could not fail?

—Unknown

When experiencing any stress in this life, it is beneficial to understand the beliefs you hold behind your stress. You form your choices by your thoughts; you form your life by your choices. It is also useful to explore the meaning behind the emotions and the words you use to describe the stress in your life.

Complete this sentence and write your response:

I feel stressed out when:

What causes stress in your life?

~ *Fear of failure?*

~ *Unmet expectations?*

~ *Fear of not doing a good job and therefore fear of judgment?*

~ *Fear that you will not be able to handle the situation?*

~ *Fear that you are not enough, just as you are?*

What is stress? If you look up the word in the dictionary, *stress* is a force that strains (for example, creates a great demand on one's emotions and resources) or deforms. You often give away the power to define whom you are to people, events, and circumstances in your life, thereby creating endless opportunities for stress.

Have you ever considered the possibility that you are complete, apart from any event or person in your life? How would that affect your daily stress level?

What emotions are behind your stress? Here are some to consider:

~ *Fear.*

~ *Embarrassment.*

~ *Vulnerability.*

~ *Invalidation.*

~ *Anger.*

~ *Worry.*

~ *Doubt.*

~ *Guilt.*

~ *Shame.*

Actually, stress is just the icing on the cake. The cake is the main emotion behind the stress, often disguised by a physical ailment (for example, back pain, headache, or neck pain). You hide your true emotions in the guise of physical pain, which is actually the physical expression of your emotional pain.

You often suppress your true emotions because you have grown up receiving messages such as: "Don't think," "don't feel," or "don't talk." Most emotional and physical problems are due to unresolved physical events that happened in your lifetime.

A "holograph" is a document written entirely in the handwriting of the person whose signature it bears. You take holographic pictures of the events in your life and then give those frozen pictures permission to define you.

All of these timeless holographs make up the matrix of your self-image. When one of your holographs is triggered (or downloaded), you explode. Afterward, you wonder, "Why did I overreact like that?" You are responding to the event at hand as if you were the age and emotional state when that holograph took place.

For example, you have a holograph from your childhood where your coach told you that you were uncoordinated and clumsy. Then, 20 years later as an adult, you are at a team-building event for work. You trip, a coworker laughingly jokes about your mishap, and you lose your temper. Your emotional response and anxiety are linked directly to that frozen moment from your past and not to the response of your coworker.

I have presented different ways to release stress in this book, so don't stress out if the concept of holographs confuses you. It's not necessary to understand the concept in order to release them.

If you take time to observe very young children, you will see that, by nature, they do not even know what stress is. Why? They do not have all of the disconnects and blocks in their body's energy system that you have created throughout your lifetime (because of your past pain in life) in order to, from your perception, survive.

When an emotion comes up in young children, it simply comes out. They continue on their way, remaining acutely present to the events at hand as well as honoring and accepting whatever emotion comes up without judgments. They don't try to analyze, interpret, or conclude as they experience life; they just experience life as it is in that moment.

As we get older and receive negative feedback on certain emotions that we freely express as children, we begin to experience stress or pressure to withhold our authentic self for fear of judgment. As adults, we forget that life is about experiences. Your emotions are meant to be experienced, not defined. You have allowed others to define your emotional state as good or bad, and acceptable or unacceptable, and you have built your sense of self-worth around other people's opinions of you.

Stress comes when you deny yourself the experience of your authentic feelings for fear of judgment. When you reconnect with your feelings and emotional state without judgment, you free yourself to love and accept all that you are, just as you are, in spite of *any* circumstance in life.

Behind the scenes of stress

"What am I afraid of?"

Behind every experience of anger is a fear. The next time you feel angry, ask yourself, "What if I fail?" Know that *your* definition of failure flows directly from your belief system (as explored in Chapter 3).

"What will other people think?"

When we worry about what other people will think, we end up becoming our own publicist and exhaust ourselves by protecting our reputation. We stress out doing daily damage control when we could be putting that energy toward learning, growing, and creating solutions.

"*What am I worried about?*"

The German word for *worry* means "to strangle" and the Greek word for *worry* means "to divide the mind." The word *doubt* means to be uncertain about something. Most of the time, stress is felt when you doubt yourself and your ability to handle a situation. Jesus spoke about the craze of worry in life: "Who of you by worrying can add a single hour to his life?" (Matthew 6:27).

"*Why can't I speak in front of that group?*"

As you will discover later in Chapter 10, you can reframe any negative statement into a positive one.

For example, you can reframe "I can't do that!" with "I just don't know how yet," or "God, guide me through this experience of self-doubt back into remembering the power that dwells within me to move mountains." This practice will help you tune into available options for solution-based outcomes.

When you wake up and realize that this world is full of opportunities for learning and growth, you will be able to connect with creative solutions to any situation in life.

You are the main judge of yourself. Forgiveness and a willingness to seek out the lessons contained in each experience on Earth are essential in order for creative thought and action to flourish within you.

"*Why do I feel disconnected and unsafe?*"

Human beings need to feel safe and connected for inspiration, creativity, and productivity to take place. Positive feedback is a powerful motivator, and it can come from within, such as personal satisfaction and affirmation, or from coworkers and reviews. When you practice remembering your worth, the world around you will also begin to recognize and respond to it.

"Why isn't this situation what I thought it would be?"

Whatever you focus on *grows bigger!* Your focus is your choice. Releasing the negative energy of unmet expectations onto which you hold when you "resist what is" gives you the opportunity to shift that energy into creative solutions and empowerment.

When you address negative thinking by trying to replace it with positive thinking, you set yourself up for resisting what is really happening. Allow yourself to feel what you feel, and then seek the grace to move through that which you are feeling. Remember your worth and capability, and they will be your guide back to inner peace.

"Why do I feel unseen, unheard, and underappreciated?"

From your perspective, these feelings may be true; however, if you choose to stay in this energy, you will remain in a state of emotional paralysis.

Your inexhaustible need for approval from the world around you is truly an addiction and becomes the ruler of your life. You will rise and fall depending on how the world judges you each day, and you will continue to feel drained, depressed, and unmotivated.

The truth is that you are enough, just as you are. You may not know it yet, or perhaps you do, but you simply forgot that you are *not* the opinions of the world around you (as discussed further in Chapter 4).

Be careful of the different faces of "playing the victim" (for example, blaming, complaining, and judging). These faces are the quickest and surest ways of remaining "stuck" in your journey of life. This behavior serves no one—especially you.

Taking full responsibility for your life leads to empowerment and speaks to this statement:

I believe I am capable of handling anything. I have full confidence in my ability to come up with creative solutions to this situation. The way to do what I want to do does exist; I simply have not yet tuned into it. Take action!

Become the watcher of your words. By your words, you define your life experience. The anxiety kicks in when your definitions of your life experience are incongruent with what is actually taking place. For example, you are turned down when you ask someone out on a date. You might take this one situation—or compare it to others in the past—and generalize your entire dating experience. This will keep you stuck in the negative mindset and you will bring that into the next situation.

When something like this happens, look at your entire time line of life, and find one or more examples that contradict your belief that nothing works out for you in dating situations. If you find one piece of information that contradicts your impoverished view of reality in any area of your life that is not "working out," you open up your ability to tune into other pieces of information from your life experience that invite you into positive perceptions.

Many times you will use universal quantifier statements such as "I never get anything done right," or "why does this always happen to me," or "nothing ever works out for me." Be careful about using these universal quantifiers, such as "always," "never," "nothing," "nobody," and "everything" to define your life experience. They produce all-or-nothing thinking, which places restrictions on your ability to access solution-based thinking.

Practice using solution-based words when faced with seemingly difficult challenges, such as "I am willing to trust in my ability to tune into all available options," or "I have moved through challenges in my past, and I am willing to trust that I can do it again."

Grab-and-Go Stress Relief Tips

~ *When you understand what you are really feeling behind the stress, this understanding gives you the opportunity to connect with a positive perception of the situation at hand, which results in creative solutions. Life is meant to be experienced, not defined. Practice letting go of your need to interpret events and allow yourself to be present in the lessons contained within the experiences. All of life contains the opportunity to expand in your ability to love.*

~ *Give yourself permission to feel any and every emotion without judgment. You used to live this way when you were young, and it is possible to revert from negative emotions back to inner peace very quickly.*

3

Messages We Get Growing Up

Whether you believe you can or you can't, you are right.

—Henry Ford

Often, I ask my clients to come up with a list of messages they learned as they were growing up. I invite them to explore the understanding that much of their stress flows from these false beliefs, which no longer serve them in life. Do any of the following messages sound familiar to you?

"In order to be loved and accepted, I need to be perfect."

Many people live in the prison of self-criticism, which usually accompanies perfectionism, and the need to be right and control situations, people, and outcomes in order to feel safe and connected.

I used to live in this prison until I was faced with death. At 38 years old, and one week prior to my final divorce court date, I was diagnosed with stage-3 breast cancer. Because of the nature of the cancer, and the extensive lymph-node involvement, I was told that I had a 50/50 chance of survival.

All of a sudden, the truth of who I am, which I forgot because of the pain and false beliefs in my life, became acutely clear to me: "I'm *not* all of those false beliefs and judgments that I have been protecting my entire life, thinking they defined who I am. I'm not my hair, breasts, or accomplishments, like getting my second-degree black belt." I began to say a daily mantra to help with the shift of self-perception:

> *Even though I believe that I need to be perfect in order to be loved and accepted, I am willing to love and accept myself anyway!*

> *Even though I'm not perfect, make mistakes, and say things I regret, I am willing to feel worthy of love and acceptance anyway. I choose to remember my worth.*

> *Even though the strength in my body is compromised because of the cancer, I am willing to remember that my greatest strength and protection flows from within my soul out through my body.*

"Don't express anger or talk back. Children are to be seen and not heard."

This type of thinking can result in repressed opinions, ideas, and creativity, which later lead to frustration, anger, and internal stress.

There is a way to speak your truth in love and integrity. Letting your feelings out comes when you embrace the truth: Your identity is not connected to the response of the world around you. As a child, you absorbed this response; as you grew up, you can realize that those responses are not who you are, nor do they define what you can or cannot do in this world—unless you give those beliefs the power to do so.

"In order to be accepted and to accept myself, I need to make a good impression."

Whose face is behind this belief? Where did you learn this? The good news is that you are the one who gives these beliefs the power to define you. Therefore, you have the power to release them.

"Don't talk unless it's nice, necessary, or kind."

This belief leads to repressed emotions, and compromises creative input and expression, which lead to insufficient productivity and less-than-creative expansion.

"Life is a struggle. Who are you to expect more in this life?"

Again, whose face is behind this question? Where did you learn this belief by which you have been living? Whatever you focus on, you tend to attract more of into your life until you see everything that comes your way through the lens of that belief. If you say to yourself, "Nothing ever works out for me," don't underestimate the power of your beliefs; they create your reality.

What messages did you learn while growing up?

List the beliefs that you adopted from the messages you picked up in your childhood. All of these messages make up the matrix of your self-image. You store these beliefs in your subconscious experience. Dr. Bruce Lipton has some powerful insight on this in his work, *The Biology of Belief*.[1]

When you have moments of overreacting, it is usually because a belief about yourself has been triggered, which you are trying to defend or about which you feel uncomfortable. It oftentimes has nothing to do with the situation at hand.

During those moments, ask yourself a few questions and then contemplate your answers:

~ *"What am I afraid of? Do I have fear of falling short? Fear of judgment? Failure? Fear that the opinions of others will define me? Am I not measuring up?"*

~ *"Does this belief serve me in my life? Have I given this belief permission to define who I am? Am I defending this belief for fear that I will not know who I am without it?"*

Remember that 95 percent of how you respond to the world around you flows from your subconscious experience—that is, beliefs about yourself and the world around you. These beliefs or tapes will continue to replay endlessly until you actually get into the energy behind the beliefs and shift the energy around new beliefs. Consider the following facts:[2]

~ *The conscious brain accounts for 17 percent of total brain mass and about one-sixth of its weight. Conversely, it controls only 2 to 4 percent of perception and behavior.*

~ *The non-conscious brain occupies 83 percent of the total brain mass and makes up the other five-sixths of its weight. But, it controls 96 to 98 percent of all perception and behavior.*

~ *Impulses in the conscious brain travel somewhere between 120 and 140 mph. Non-conscious impulses travel at more than 100,000 mph, which is roughly 800 times faster than conscious impulses.*

~ *"Information in the conscious brain is processed at the rate of around 2,000 bits per second. The nonconscious brain processes information at four hundred billion bits per second."*

In Chapter 12, we discuss an energy technique that will help you make the shift. For now, increase your awareness of the beliefs about yourself and the world around you that have led to your impoverished view of reality.

Take action

The next time you identify a negative belief or agreement that you made in your lifetime, remember that you are the one who created that agreement or belief. The good news is that this means that you are capable of creating a new agreement that promotes a positive self-image.

For example, one of my clients had an experience as a young boy. His father offered expressions of support and love, but only after accomplishing or achieving something. He created an internal agreement that sounded something like this: "In order to receive love and acceptance, I need to accomplish, excel, and succeed in this life." This statement resulted in the belief that whatever he did was not good enough. He had to change the energy around that belief and create a new agreement so that one day it would be enough to know himself as loved and accepted, just as he is.

These types of agreements lead to the use of modal operators of necessity ("must" and "can't" thinking), which indicate a lack of choice, such as "*I must* keep working," "I *have to* finish this project," or "It's *necessary* that I accomplish this."

We say these things in order to love and accept ourselves, just as we are. A very powerful response to this type of thinking would be to ask yourself: "What would happen if I *did* stop working? What would happen if I *didn't* finish this project or accomplish this task?" Your answers will achieve a fuller model of reality, once again giving you the opportunity to tune into all available options along with a more complete representation of your world.

Before I lost my hair, the thought of seeing myself bald and breastless at 38 years old panicked me. Since I was about to start dating again for the first time in 17 years, I concluded that no one would want to date a woman who was bald and breastless.

Many nights, I thought to myself, "I *have to* figure out a way to keep my hair."

In spite of my determination, all of my hair fell out 14 days after my first chemo treatment. One week before that experience, I adjusted my agreement of "In order to feel confident about myself in dating situations, I need to have my hair and breasts" to "I am willing to love and accept myself with or without hair and breasts. I choose to remember that God has created me in beauty and love, and I will radiate that to those around me."

In 2009, I married a man I had a crush on in college. Here is a segment of the conversation we had on our first date, as I boldly shared my truth:

"I have learned to be very transparent. I can tell that I really like you, so this is where I am at in my life. I am bald (I was wearing a wig) and breastless. I just went through a divorce one year ago and was diagnosed with cancer. I have three children, and I am going through a ton of surgeries as they graft my back onto my front because of third-degree burns all over my chest from the chemo/radiation combination. I just need to know if all of this is a deal-breaker."

After a very long sideways glance at my wig, he replied, "Don't worry about it. That is a sweet-looking wig, and I am a leg and butt man."

That response got him a second date and my love for the rest of his life.

Give yourself permission to be real, and love all that you are, just as you are. Then, go for what you want in this life.

Grab-and-Go Stress Relief Tips

~ *Explore the inner list of requirements of love and accepting yourself that you have been gathering your entire life, which could also be known as "the writing on your walls." You are not the writing on your wall. At any point, you can choose to move through the messages you received in life back into the truth of who you are: loved, safe, connected, capable, alive, and inspired!*

~ *Stress occurs when you think that your impoverished view of reality is who you truly are. As you recover lost pieces of information about yourself, you expand your options and possibilities.*

4

Attachment and Happiness

When you change the way you look at things, the things you look at change. If I am what I do, when I don't...I'm not.

—Dr. Wayne Dyer

Anthony de Mello's book, *The Way to Love*, speaks the simple truth. An "attachment" is an emotional state of clinging caused by the belief that, without some particular thing or person, you cannot be happy.[1]

Attachment contains two elements:

1. *The thrill you experience when you get what you are attached to.*

2. *The anxiety that always accompanies the attachment for fear that one may lose it.*

You waste so much energy in life striving for happiness, and say, "If I can only lose this weight, then I will be happy," or "If I could only make this amount of money, then I will be happy." During my experience with cancer, I remember thinking, at a low moment, "If I weren't bald and breastless, I would be happy and able to handle this."

You think, "If I can get this one thing, then I will be happy." *This is not true.* As mentioned previously, the anxiety quickly follows the thrill of getting what you want in life for fear that you may lose it. This vicious life cycle will be broken when you remember the extent of God's love for you, and your true worth flows from that remembering.

Complete the two powerful statements, which will reveal your attachments:

~ *I am okay with:*

~ *I am okay without:*

If you feel anxiety and stress inside when you speak the word *without*, then you know you have an attachment.

Some people have said, "Well, I'm *not* okay without this particular thing or person." Great! Brutal honesty is the first step to healing false beliefs.

When your journey on Earth ends, you will find that you have always been okay. You simply forgot along the way, and perhaps you might even regret the energy you wasted trying to own, control, possess, analyze, interpret, and conclude, along with all of the striving, which stemmed from your need for certain outcomes in order for you to feel loved, accepted, safe, capable, validated, and connected.

A moment of enlightenment came when I surveyed my naked body in front of the mirror after my mastectomy. At the time, I was bald and breastless. The scars on my chest seemed to go on for all of eternity. At that moment, I remembered *me.* I realized, "I'm not my breasts. I'm not my hair. I'm not these scars on my chest."

Who I am existed apart from all that was outside of me. I realized how powerful this shift in perception was going to be in my life:

If I am not all of the outer things to which I have attached my sense of self and my sense of happiness in life, then I am truly FREE to be happy all of the time. I can express my ideas, thoughts, and inspirations without worrying about what other people will think. I am loved, safe, and okay, no matter what surrounds me. This is going to be fun! I am truly returning to the curious and fascinated parts of life that I once knew as a child!

Remember that you are always happy; you just forget this fact when you farm out your sense of identity to the world around you. You came into this world with everything you need for life and happiness; you came in naked, without clutching anything in your hands.

Have you ever noticed that, when young children play, they don't take things personally? Oh, yes, they will express their feelings about things, but they don't linger in judgments or opinions of their peers as adults do. They just keep on being who they are and express all that they are without analyzing their thoughts or actions. They connect to the happiness within themselves and their God-given ability to "be."

All of the spiritual wisdom that has come to us through the ages speaks to the truth that happiness dwells within you, not outside of you. Your thoughts are the greatest source of your unhappiness. Release the negative thinking and *you will remember that you are happy.* Happiness always flows from the inside out   not the outside in.

I remember when I was first diagnosed with cancer, I was told that I had about a 50/50 chance of survival—statistically speaking. Contemplating my own death, all that was essential in my life had its way with me over the nonessential.

At that moment, an energy shift took place instantly, and the realization emerged within my soul that spoke to this truth:

I keep forgetting that I am always okay and able to handle any situation that enters my life—even death. My fears, doubts, and worries are simply an illusion based on my false perception that I am not okay and I won't be able to handle this. I don't have to strive anymore to try to change things and people by trying to own, control, and possess that which is before me in order to know that I am okay, just as I am—and it's time to remember that. This cancer is a gift of remembrance of all I forgot in my life that is essential and infinite.

Releasing attachments

Complete this statement, taking time to reflect on the details and elements involved:

I will be happy when:

Awareness is essential for the shift to take place. You now have a list of what you believe you need in order to be happy. Take each attachment and see it for what it really is: the cause of your unhappiness for fear that you may lose it or never be happy.

Here is a new perception for you to contemplate:

Even though I think I need this, that, or the other thing in my life in order to be happy, I choose to be happy with or without it.

Take back the power you give to people and things to make you happy. Remember that you are happy simply being you—alive, beautiful, capable, and connected to God.

Your human energy field goes out 10 feet and 360 degrees around you and beyond. Happiness releases the tension in your energy field, which changes the world around you—at work and at home. Try it! Love evokes love and anger evokes anger. You have the choice. By your choices, you form your life. *Choose wisely!*

Lateral communication in the corporate world and at home involves connection, whether it is positive or negative. Notice how your connections with people change when you choose to connect to the experience of happiness apart from attachments, response, or mood of those around you. You will notice that, as you choose to embrace the higher vibration of love, gratitude, and integrity, your world will lighten up. As you remember your worth, those around you also will begin to recognize and respond to it.

A powerful daily mantra is: "I am okay with or without this." *Go for it!* You will notice that, when you release the tension caused by needing something in order to feel okay about you, you have an endless supply of energy to put toward creative ideas and solutions to any situation at hand.

The energy from your mind goes out 2 inches. This is where unhappiness stems from when you worry that you may not be okay if you don't get this, that, or the other thing in your life.

Heart-based living is essential for a stress-free life. Drop out of your head and into your heart. The mind needs to constantly calculate and define life, pulling from past and future events that are nonexistent except by perception only.

The heart experiences life without the need to define it. This is the place where creativity, expansion, and freedom flourish. Know the expansive energy that flows when you move from your heart out into the world. Explore removing the phrase "I think" and replacing it with "I feel."

I will end this section with a saying I learned in youth group growing up. I posted it on my mirror throughout the cancer treatments:

Without God, I am nothing, with God I am everything, and ALL things are possible for me in my life.

I added this:

I choose life and love NO MATTER WHAT surrounds me today. Authentic happiness flows from the inside out—no exceptions.

Take action

Fast from negative thinking this week. One of your greatest strengths lies in your ability to control the act of labeling your thoughts as threatening. As life unfolds before you, you have thoughts about what you experience or encounter. These thoughts can remain in a place of simple observation or take on the ability to create an emotion—good or bad—depending on the labels you use.

As soon as you label a thought as threatening (that is, you will not be okay in some way, shape, or form), you give birth to a negative emotion such as fear, doubt, or worry. The fuel behind these emotions usually comes down to this type of thought: "I'm not okay" or "I won't be able to handle this."

Your greatest ability to tune into all available options for solution-based thinking flows directly from a place of remembering that *no matter what happens,* you have the God-given ability to handle it *and* you are always okay.

A moment in my own life offers a great illustration for this truth. My 10-year-old son walked in to my room and found me weeping on my knees after I had lost all of my hair to chemo. He snuck up behind me and put his little hands on my head.

"Mom, don't cry. Your soul still has hair!"

Instantly, I stopped crying and asked him to repeat that wisdom.

You can apply this truth to all of life. No matter what threat you feel at any single moment in life, remember your natural, God-given state of being: "You are safe and complete in God, lacking nothing." When you seek that which is already within and around you, it is as if you are asking a fish if he knows where the water is. Wake up and release all of your attachments to the outside things that you think will make you happy.

I invite you to be the gatekeeper of your thoughts. Watch as a thought comes out of the gate. As you practice remaining curious and fascinated about *all* of life, you stay in that expansive realm of creative thinking linked directly to your ability to maintain creative problem-solving abilities.

As soon as you label a thought as a negative threat in any way, you shut down the flow of life through you. Life is meant to be experienced, which involves flexibility and flow, and is not defined. As soon as you define anything, you confine it to that definition. Rather than saying, "I can't do that," try saying, "This is an opportunity to tap into a new ability or talent." Perhaps the opportunity is to learn to overcome a new situation in which you feel threatened.

Expand your ability to live life without the fear, doubt, and worry. This ability starts with fasting from negative thoughts. It's truly amazing how much room you create in your head when you clean out the negative thought patterns.

Grab-and-Go Stress Relief Tips

~ *You are not what you have attached yourself to in this world. Who you are exists apart from the material world. Embracing this truth will result in happiness, which does not rise and fall depending on the world around you. The need to own, control, and possess things or people equals stress.*

~ *Have one attachment: your heart to God's love within and around you.*

~ *When you remember your true worth, you will stop your antics of attachment to things outside of you for your sense of well-being and inner peace.*

5

Your Inner List for Love and Acceptance

Once you have farmed out your sense of identity to the words or reactions in the world around you, the response you get becomes a part of your "inner wall." Your sense of well-being and inner feelings of "I'm okay" are now linked directly to the reaction you got from the world around you.

Here are some common messages:

~ *I am okay if I am perfect.*

~ *I don't talk.*

~ *I am fit.*

~ *I am recognized.*

~ *I can lead.*

~ *I can manage my life.*

~ *I can do it all.*

~ *I drive a nice car.*

~ *I make a lot of money.*

~ *I finish what I start.*

~ *I keep everything organized and neat.*

~ *I am thin.*

~ *I am fat.*

~ *I hold in what I'm really feeling.*

~ *I don't talk back.*

~ *I do talk back.*

~ *I stay small in life.*

~ *I am at the top.*

~ *I don't ask for too much.*

~ *People say that I am okay.*

~ *People affirm me.*

~ *People validate me.*

~ *People accept me and love me.*

~ *I am always right.*

~ *I control people.*

~ *People listen to me and do what I say.*

~ *People do things the way I do things.*

~ *I own things.*

~ *I possess the ability to micromanage my life.*

~ *I work and don't play.*

~ *I am in a relationship.*

These statements do not hold any power to define you unless you give the power to them. Once you give the statement power to define you and "make you happy" (as mentioned in Chapter 4), that statement becomes a part of the inner list that represents who you think you are or need to be in order to be worthy of love and acceptance, often referred to as the "writing on your wall."

You become enslaved and addicted to the attachment cycle. You become vulnerable to stress and victimization. You rise and fall emotionally in your life based on your inner list or requirements to feel okay about yourself. You become stressed because you fear that you are not okay without checking off your inner list. Again, the truth is that *you are always okay*. You just forget when you give power to "the wall" to define who you are.

Take back your power

How do you take your power back? Ask yourself these questions and record your answers:

~ *What do you need to happen around you in order for you to accept yourself, just as you are?*

~ *What needs to shift within your life perspective in order for you to wake up in the morning knowing that you are enough, just as you are?*

~ *What do you need in order to know or remember your God-given talents and capabilities?*

~ *What do you need to remember or know in order to love yourself completely?*

~ *Knowing that a sense of prosperity comes from remembering your worth, what do you need around you to feel successful?*

Then, make three lists, writing your answers with thoughtful consideration:

1. *In order to accept me, I need (ruthless honesty):*
2. *In order to love me (or in order to feel loved), I need:*
3. *In order to feel successful or prosperous (and that I have made it in this life), I need:*

The next time you are triggered into stress, see if the situation is connected to any of the beliefs that you wrote down. Remember: It's okay to want certain outcomes in life; just don't attach your sense of self-worth to them. For example, when you experience comparison or jealousy toward another person, you feel threatened. You feel that he or she has something you need in order to love and accept yourself. This momentary amnesia comes from forgetting your unique beauty and worth in this world. Accept and love *yourself* no matter what surrounds you.

When you feel anxious within, check the lists you have made and call yourself out, stand eye to eye with the requirements you are referencing in order to love and accept yourself, and say to that requirement, "I see you for what you are, and I choose a new agreement with myself in this moment." This new agreement is not based on a list of requirements, but on my natural God-infused state of being, which says, "I am enough, just as I am. I am worthy and capable, and unconditionally loved by God for the purpose of inspiring to create beauty and love in this world."

Awareness is the key to writing new messages on your walls that are in line with the truth: You are okay no matter what surrounds you, just as you are. This is a journey of remembrance and recovery. Remember who you are, apart from all attachments and reactions from the world around you, and recover those pieces of information about yourself that you simply forgot along the way as you farmed out your sense of identity to the world around you.

You have often conveyed to people, "You tell me if I am enough, if I am capable and whole, and if I am worthy of being heard and seen in this world. Whatever you tell me, I will make an agreement with it, and this information will make up the lens through which I see myself in this world."

Release this madness and take back your God-given ability to remember and step into the fullness of the magnificent human being you were created to be—one thought at a time. As you make this transition back into *you*, practice being a curious and fascinated human being. You will remember how powerful it feels when you are in the place of observation versus reactive unconscious responses to life. It actually becomes quiet humorous as you witness the little antics you play in order to be seen, acknowledged, and recognized.

Remember: Stress is simply a signal within your body giving you the opportunity to identify and adjust your perception of people, things, and circumstances. *Lighten up!* This is all the practice of remembering *you* and your natural state of being. It's easier than you think because this practice exists beyond thought.

Take action

If you want to create positive relationships in your life, begin with yourself. This sounds like a redundant statement, and it's probably not the first time you have heard it. Practice releasing assumptions about what other people think or why they do what they do in your life.

You see people and respond to their actions based on how you see yourself. You know this to be true. Think back on the last few weeks, and pick out a time when you were feeling good about yourself, confident, and playful.

Consider these questions:

~ *How did a lighthearted response to life affect your perceptions of the people around you?*

~ *Did you let things roll off your back?*

~ *Did you release others from your judgments when they did not respond the way you wanted them to?*

~ *Did you experience a momentary hiatus from taking everything personally?*

If you experienced a positive shift in your perception of those around you once, you can do it again. The choice of response to life is yours, and your choice makes a difference in the outcome.

You see others as you see yourself. As you increase love and grace toward yourself, you will offer the same to those around you. Are you stuck in relationships? Begin within. Take time to connect with the love of God, which you have experienced many times in sunsets, laughter, love from animals, birds singing, and connections with those whom you love.

Let go of mind-reading, assuming that you know what other people are thinking and why they do what they do. If you are missing pieces of information on any interpersonal connection, simply ask for more details or clarity. Then, dismantle statements of assumption, which keep you stuck in your head, such as "He doesn't understand me," to which I would reply, "How specifically do you know that he does not understand you?" This response will challenge you to question your assumptions and seek further information that perhaps you take for granted.

Grab-and-Go Stress Relief Tips

~ *Explore your list of inner requirements: What do you believe you must do or be in order to love and accept yourself just as you are? Once you bring this list into the light by writing it down, you are more equipped to remember that you are enough just as you are.*

~ *Remind yourself of this list of requirements in order to love and accept yourself, just as you are, every time you encounter a response from the world around you that triggers one of the items on your list. For example, if you wrote on your inner list of requirements that you need to be perfect in order to be loved, then any time a situation occurs around you that speaks to imperfection, you will be triggered into stress.*

6

Mental Muck Fuels the Procrastination Rut

To procrastinate in life is to create unnecessary stress in your body. How many times have you put off something that you don't want to do, yet you feel that you need to do it, such as paying taxes or bills, making sales calls, confronting relationship issues, organizing your home or work space, or creating your next speech, book, presentation, or business plan?

What do you put off in your life that you feel you need to do in order to keep things running smoothly, or to expand and move your next project forward? Why do you keep pushing back the next step toward accomplishing your desired goal? Perhaps you might say, "If I knew the answer to that, I wouldn't be reading this chapter!"

Let's take a look at a few possible reasons why you procrastinate or put things off that you feel you need to do yet don't do, and the more you don't do them, the more pressure and stressed out you feel, along with guilt for not doing those things you feel you need to do but don't. *Whew!*

When you do not align yourself with what you value the most—which, by the way, is your God-given, natural state of being that fuels your sense of purpose—you become vulnerable to distractions and fragmentation, which gives birth to the frustration of procrastination.

More often than not, distractions flow from unbridled ambitions and vanity. With the drug of approval, for example, the need to be acknowledged, seen, recognized, and approved of will fragment your ability to move forward and will lead to procrastination (that is, putting off an action around a highly valued project for a task of lesser value).

Unbridled ambitions and vanity are based on desires, expectations, assumptions, and a sense of entitlement rather than on worth and what *you* value in this life. These flow from what you *think* you need in order to feel accomplished and successful. They are phantom pursuits that distract you from the clarity of focus needed to complete your God-inspired life projects.

These unbridled ambitions often create a muck of thoughts, which are tied up around an internal list of expectations that you have created and use as a benchmark around feeling accomplished in this life. For example, "I will accept myself if..." If *what*? If you accomplish your to-do list today or create and implement a successful business plan?

This type of thinking can create a belief system that sounds something like this: "In order to love and accept myself completely and unconditionally, I need to be perfect." Don't be fooled. Perfectionism and procrastination walk hand in hand: "If I do what I want or feel that I need to do, and the end result is not perfect, then I have failed. So, to avoid the emotions and experience of failure, I will put this project off for a while. In this way, I'm safe."

This is not the case for all procrastination. However, the face of perfectionism often creeps below the murky surface of the *putting-things-off rut*, and it's worth your attention. Look your perfectionism program right in the eyes and make a mental shift as you remember that you are enough just as you are, doing or not doing. Then, go for what you want and you will not attach yourself to the outcome. Releasing all attachment to a certain outcome will ignite your ability to create and expand more quickly than a lit match in a dry haystack.

I learned The More, The More NLP technique from the founder of the American University of NLP, Steve G. Jones. It is used to create a mental association between two unrelated thoughts. You are making thousands of mental associations every several minutes, so why not be the gatekeeper of those associations and take them captive for your greater good?

The next time you find yourself accomplishing a lot in your mind, yet not taking action to make these things happen, use this technique:

~ *The More (state your thought).*

~ *The More (state your action).*

For example: "The more I think about putting off this project, the more motivated I feel to take action on my next step to move my project forward."

I have successfully used The More, The More technique at night, and here are the words I have used many times to fall into a deep sleep: "The more my mind keeps me up, the more I am able to surrender all thoughts and wonderings to God, and relax into a deep, peaceful sleep, easily and naturally."

When you align yourself with what you value most and move from your God connection—from the inside out rather than the outside in—you experience excitement, which results in motivation and action-based behavior.

As you become aware of some of the possible fuels behind your procrastination situation, you will expand your ability to realize that you are not a victim. You have the ability to take the necessary action to kick-start your motivation and move ahead in life.

Here is an overview of a few reasons why you might procrastinate:

~ **You fear failure and think that the result will not be good enough.** *It won't measure up to your internal list of items, such as "I will feel accomplished when...." As a result, you put off taking positive action toward completing and implementing your project. "What if it's not good enough? What if people don't like it? What if I'm not an expert? Why should people listen and be inspired by me?" Self-doubt rises up, and the solutions are positive self-image and self-efficacy. It is the belief that you are called to do what you are doing, and that you have all of the skills and talents to do it—if it is aligned with your God-given natural state of being, along with motives that flow from what you value most in life. In this space, creating is like breathing: unrestricted and in the flow.*

~ **Your negative feelings around attachment lead to fragmented behavior.** *"I need this to work out in order to be happy, accept myself, and feel successful, loved, and enough." This is an emotional state of being because of the belief that, without some thing, person, or situation, you can't be happy. This state is enough to keep you stagnant because you don't want the negative feelings if you don't get it. Your desire* *to get it launched is misaligned, which gives birth to fragmented behavior. You can't stay on task because you are too distracted by your need for a certain outcome. The fear that you won't get it is enough to cause you not to even try.*

~ **You think that what you are setting out to accomplish is not aligned with what you value most in life.** *Ask yourself, "Why do I want to launch this program?" You might say, "Because I can share my knowledge." Knowledge is simply a transfer of information; however, if you put out information in this world and create a positive experience, which will lead people to a more fulfilled physical, emotional, or spiritual life, it is life enhancing and it will attract others People look for experiences where their senses—looks like, feels like, sounds like—are engaged. Be specific about the goals you want to accomplish, even if it is something like cleaning the house. The more specific you become in terms of the core motivating factors behind your goals, the more likely you are to take action around them. Whatever your goal is, say, "I want to accomplish this specific goal so I can ("feel," "experience," "go beyond," "realize," "become aware of," "move beyond my limitations around," "explore," or "because if I do, then…"). Clear focus leads to clear responses in life.*

Explore the personal benefits of accomplishing your goal to yourself and others. Focus on doing what you do because you *want* to, not because you *need* to. Avoid guilt words, such as "need" and "have to." Guilt will keep you stuck.

To supercharge your energy behind a project, find the elements that excite you and anchor them, as described in the Godiva Chocolate Pattern by Richard Bandler, one of the original founders of NLP. I learned this technique during my training with Steve G. Jones (founder of the American University of NLP) for my NLP Master Certification. NLP, Neuro Linguistic Programming, is the systematic study of human performance and known for its ability to create expansive inner transformation leading to personal excellence. Known for its subjective component, NLP techniques can be modified and adjusted for each individual according to their life experience and perceptions giving therapists the opportunity to initiate positive shifts and beneficial behavior in the lives of his or her clients. I have witnessed quick and lasting behavioral shifts and mental perspectives, as a result of using NLP with my clients. The use of anchors, as described following this paragraph, gives you the ability to resurrect a desired behavior to the front lines of your emotional response to life and therefore your behavior. As you think of what you don't like or don't want to do and anchor that in your biology with something you do like, your behavior will shift toward the positive:

1. *Close your eyes and create a picture of something that you love to do, something that evokes positive feelings and that you are compelled to do naturally and easily because you want to. Imagine what it feels like, sounds like, and looks like while doing the thing that you love to do. Increase your sensory experience using your imagination. The conscious mind does not know the difference between what is real and imaginary when you engage your sensory awareness. When you feel that you are close to the peak of your sensory experience as you*

imagine this thing you love to do, reach over and touch the inside of your arm, just above your wrist (either hand will work). This creates a physical Anchor 1, which links to your emotional experience of doing that which you love to do.

2. *Open your eyes and then close them.*

3. *Create a picture of something that you feel you need to do but don't like doing, like paying bills or cleaning the house. It should be something that you find easy to procrastinate on. Imagine yourself watching you do this task. Reach over and touch the inside of your arm, just below your elbow, creating Anchor 2 on the same arm you used for Anchor 1 in Step 1.*

4. *You have now created two physical anchors associated with two different tasks and emotional states.*

5. *Bring up the picture from Step 1 and hold Anchor 1 (the spot just above your wrist on the inside of your arm). As you see that picture of you doing what you love, imagine fading that image as you bring up the picture associated with Anchor 2 (the picture of you doing what you tend to procrastinate). Reach over and touch the inside of your arm, just below your elbow of the same arm, which is An-chor 2.*

6. *Hold both anchors simultaneously. Use your thumb to hold Anchor 2, reach across the inside of your arm, and press on Anchor 1 (below your wrist).*

7. *You have now associated something you don't like doing and are apt to procrastinate on with something you do like to do. Repeat this exercise to strengthen the association between these two activities.*

Infuse the things you don't like to do with personal value in order to jump-start your motivation. Look beyond the task to the bigger purpose of your efforts. Verbally associate what you don't want to do with what you do want to experience. For example, if you don't like to organize because it does not come easily to you, say, "The more I put off organizing around this project, the more motivated I become to take a positive step toward infusing my life with order and simplicity." Feel free to add, "Even though I have identified with the struggle in my life, I choose to take action around my desired goals, easily and naturally." Your brain has the ability to create a new association instantaneously; you simply forget that you have the ability to program it.

Take action

Many things can create fragmented thinking throughout your day, which can lead to procrastination. Overwhelm leads to lack of focus and lack of productivity. Ask these questions and say these statements as you tap on your thymus, located 2 inches down from the U-shaped dip in your neck:

~ *"Even though I feel fragmented in my thinking and unproductive today, I am willing to love and accept myself."*

~ *"What if I could be really clear in my thinking in the midst of my to-do list? What would I need to remember or feel in order to make this possible for me? I choose to trust in my ability to easily experience focus and purpose in the work I do or don't do today."*

Apply an NLP kinesthetic swish technique I learned in my NLP training program with Steve G. Jones. As you look up to the right and tap on your thymus, say these statements:

~ *"I choose to surprise myself at how easily I am able to maintain clarity of focus and calm, no matter how many projects I have in front of me today."*

~ *"I am willing to easily expand my ability to ground myself in what I value most as I connect with my purpose, and easily and naturally accomplish my goals today. I am now able to experience an unlimited awareness of focus that leads to accurate responses all day long."*

Tap, tap, tap, tap, and take three deep breaths. Now, realize your clarity of focus and go for what you want!

Another tip

Procrastination can keep you from implementing a high-powered project. The next time you feel like resisting, take a small step forward toward completing your project, and then stop and consider organizing one corner of your office space or three files associated with the project you are working on.

Fragmentation due to disorganization leads to procrastination. When you take a step in the direction of organization around a project, even if it is a small corner of organization, you will find that you create simplicity. Simplicity leads to clarity of focus, and clarity of focus leads to action-based living. Remember: This is the popular program often associated with procrastination: "In order to accept myself, I need to be perfect. I am resisting taking a step toward completing this project for fear of possible rejection by myself or by those around me."

Perfectionism and procrastination often walk hand in hand. Reflect on this statement: "I am willing to accept myself and honor my unique creativity with or without accomplishing this project." You will find that you often release new energy to move forward when you remember you are okay just as you are.

A wise author once asked, "What would you dare to do if you knew that you could not fail?" That person understood a key element that needs to be in place before advancement could happen. The ability to create can only take place in the presence of freedom.

Use this tip to expand motivation in the midst of the mundane. Singleness of heart creates focus and motivation in life. Run your race in such a way as to get the prize—that which you value most in this life, those things that expand your experience of love, joy, peace, happiness, patience, kindness, playfulness, goodness, gentleness, self-control, integrity, and more love.

What do you value most in this life? Take a moment, right now, to write down five things you value most in your life. Clarity of focus leads to accuracy of response. When you spend time thinking about, spending time with, and pursuing what you value most, you will experience more of it in your life.

Whatever you choose to do in this world, give it 100 percent of your effort, even if you find yourself in a place of transition or mundane moments. When you put forth 100 percent toward that which you happen to be doing now, the doors to creativity, opportunity, and possibilities will swing open.

Watch out for the serpent of greed in your life. Greed has many different faces and the ability to render you paralyzed, unable to move forward and expand your influence in this world. It begins with excessive comparison, which flows from the fear that another person has something you need in order to love and accept yourself ("feel accomplished," "enough," or "capable"). Unmanaged, it quickly turns into "hubris," which means "1. pride or arrogance" or "2. an excess of ambition, pride, etc., ultimately causing the transgressor's ruin."[1]

Sound familiar? Perhaps you have witnessed this dragon's face in yourself or those around you: excessive ambition that pursues its own advancement and personal gain in life—in spite of the values it may abandon, including love, kindness, service, and humility, in order to grip onto more acknowledgment, recognition, and/or possessions.

You may say, "I don't have that." Yet, I challenge you to observe the different choices you make throughout your day. Look behind the actions you choose to make. Do you put things above people? Do you put people above things? What is the fuel behind what you do in this life?

By now, you have explored many different emotions and reactions to life and the responses you get. Sometimes the dragon of hubris has become so ingrained in the small acts you do or tone of voice you use that it flies below your conscious radar.

Wake up and observe what motivates you to do what you do with the moments of life with which you have been blessed. After two near-death experiences during my two years of intense treatment for advanced cancer, I can assure you that these reflections will stand on the front lines of your conscious mind at the end of your life on earth.

Align all aspects of *you* with what you value most in life, release the grip of hubris (excessive ambition), and watch your world regain the wonderment and curious exploration that captivated you as a child.

With each new dawn, I take time to connect with God first, knowing that all good and purpose-filled actions and responses flow from that connection out through me to those around me.

The following is a prayer I use for motivation, which is grounded in worth and value:

God, have Your way with me in spite of myself for a greater good in my life and in the lives of those around me. Inspire me to take action easily and naturally on those projects, tasks, and personal and professional goals that bring about that which is good, right, sincere, beautiful, excellent, and full of love, compassion, and reverence for all of life. Fill me with a spirit of joy and laughter so I will have fun doing what You call me to do in this world.

Grab-and-Go Stress Relief Tips

~ *When you use The More, The More NLP technique, it creates positive verbal associations for statements that keep you stuck. For example:*

~ *"The more I feel unmotivated, the more clarity I am able to access in terms of tuning in and taking action on my next step forward."*

~ *"The more I procrastinate doing this task, the easier it is for me to step out of the mental muck and tune into action-based thinking."*

~ *"The more I feel unmotivated and unfocused, the more I am able to activate my ability to jump into action and clarity of focus."*

7

When Priorities Are Clear, Decisions Are Easy

When I was 16, I began to study the works of Leo Buscaglia, known as "Dr. Love." One of Leo's statements has resonated with me since I first read it as a teenager: "People before things."

I have continued to say this statement every morning before starting my day. When I am faced with this decision in my day—things or people—I am reminded of the decision I made as a youth to put people before things. Giving people my time and attention before material things is something I highly value and want to live by. Do I always honor people above my "things to do" list? Absolutely *not*. However, my anxiety increases when I don't because I am moving against what I believe is important to me in life; any time I do that, anxiety enters.

What do you value most in life?

People experience a lot of stress over making everyday decisions. When you are trying to make a decision, you are focusing on your options: "Am I going to do this or that? Which one am I going to choose?"

Your decision will become clear when you connect your options to your priorities and to what you value most in this life. It's similar to the exercise when you lose something and start to look everywhere in a panic to find what you lost. When you slow down and retrace your steps, you usually find that item.

Frustration and anxiety often come when the things you do in life conflict with your priorities. If family is a priority, and you continue to get business calls after hours, anxiety will build. Oftentimes, you just plow through the anxiety, you take the call, and your children quietly go upstairs. You miss the opportunity to connect and honor one of your priorities in life, resulting in frustration and anxiety.

The key factor here is to become aware of your priorities. What is important to you in life? What do you value most? You only have one life and it goes by *fast*. Where do you want to spend your time and energy each day? Know what you value and then make time for it each day. Even if you devote just a little time, *do it*.

When you reflect at the end of the day on the things that moved you, which is a worthwhile practice to connect you to love and inspiration, clarity will arise around those things you highly value.

Try this practice for three days and record those moments that have lingered in your heart by writing them down, regardless of whether or not they produce a positive or negative charge in your body.

~ *Day 1—These events moved me today:*

~ *Day 2—These events moved me today:*

~ *Day 3—These events moved me today:*

As you practice tuning consciously into those things that move you, you will be able to notice more of what moves you throughout your days. You are only bumped within (that is, inspired or vexed) when the event has triggered something of value to you, such as your reputation, your ability to connect with others, or your experience as a parent, spouse, or friend.

Remember that those things you value most in life more often than not flow from your experience of connection along with your feelings of safety—or lack of it—within those connections: with God, yourself, and those around you. Reflect for a moment on what you value most in life.

This will give you the opportunity to reflect upon those areas that may have become distorted due to fear and false beliefs, which are usually fueled by the "I will love and accept myself when..." way of thinking.

Imagine you believe that you have already *made it* in this life, and that you are loved and accepted by God, just as you are. How would imagining that help you remember what you truly value in this life?

Pull from your previous recordings the moments that moved you, and caused you to stop, linger, listen, and look. Write down—with no judgment—what you observe to be important to you in life. Release all sense of what you feel that you *should* value and have a moment of ruthless honesty. Reflect on your words daily, perhaps using the phrase "What do I value most in life?" as your screen saver, or someplace you will see it often.

Rules for the discernment of spirits

Here is some wisdom on decision-making from one of the great spiritual teachers of history: *Rules for the Discernment of Spirits*, by St. Ignatius of Loyola:[1]

~ **Intellect.** *Analyze the situation logically. What are the advantages and disadvantages of each course of action? Do the advantages of one choice substantially outweigh the other choices? Which decision seems best from a rational point of view?*

~ **Feelings.** *What feelings, if any, are raised as you consider each possibility? Is there a strong sense of desire or excitement involved in one option (which may be an indication it should be chosen) or sense of dread or unhappiness over another (which may indicate that this choice is not God's will for you)?*

~ **Imagination.** *If someone came to you for advice about the situation you were facing, what would you say or urge that person to do? If you imagined yourself on your deathbed looking back at all the choices and actions of your lifetime, and knowing that you'd soon be reviewing them with God, what decision—from that perspective—would you want to have made?*

According to St. Ignatius, after you go through one or more of these steps, a course of action will usually begin to stand out from the rest.

Take action

Some of the most powerful techniques that I have used in my own life have come from my certification training in NLP, the systematic study of human performance. Some of the pioneers in the NLP methods include Richard Bandler, John Grinder, and Robert Dilts. Virginia Satir, Milton Erickson, and Gregory Bateson explored and expanded on the practical application of the NLP methodology.

In addition, Polish-American scientist and one of NLP's pioneers, Alfred Habdank Skarbek Korzybski, said, "God may forgive you for your sins, but your nervous system won't." This explains why you may embrace the belief of forgiveness yet your neurology holds onto the trauma of events that have occurred in your past, resulting in phobias, addictions, low self-esteem, and impoverished thinking. Korzybski believed that NLP was an integration of psychology, linguistics, neurology, cybernetics, and systems theory.

The main goal of NLP is to teach people how to learn, motivate, and change their behavior, thus creating excellence and spiritual, emotional, and physical congruency. NLP techniques create positive shifts in focus, expanding your ability to tune into all available options and leading to creative problem-solving.

NLP is the science of shift. It explains how you take in information from your life experiences through your five senses of hearing, sight, touch, smell, and taste (neuro); how you give meaning to, process, code, and organize the information you take in and transform the information into language (linguistic), and how you create programs based on the information you take in and organize (programming).

To create congruency and alignment for any desired emotional, spiritual, and physical shifts in life, the NLP Logical Levels of Change—inspired by Gregory Bateson's work, and expanded by Robert Dilts and other NLP pioneers—are worth exploring. They are useful when you are seeking to align yourself and the work you are doing in this world with what you value most in this life.

You are more likely to achieve your desired outcome as you create congruency in the following areas:

~ **Spiritual/Vision:** *What is the bigger purpose for your desired outcome? How does your desired outcome benefit other people? Will it create a greater good? How so?*

~ **Actions:** *What actions will you take to accomplish your desired outcome? What will you do?*

~ **Values:** *Is this desired outcome aligned with your beliefs and with what you value most in life? Why is having this outcome important to you?*

~ **Identity:** *Is this desired outcome aligned with who you are?*

~ **Capabilities:** *What God-given gifts and talents will you need to use or access in order to achieve your desired outcome?*

~ **Environment:** *Where, when, and with whom will you create this desired outcome?* [2]

Take time this week to make a list of 10 things you value most in life. As new goals emerge throughout the week, give yourself permission to step back from the "doing" aspects of accomplishing those goals. Reflect on how those goals align with what you value most. Think about your God-given talents and skills, who you are, who is in alignment with what you value most in life, and the greater good that will result in your life and the lives of others when you complete your desired outcome. Practicing this reflection process in your life will create congruency within—spiritually, emotionally, and physically—and result in clarity of focus, productivity, and a sense of purpose.

Grab-and-Go Stress Relief Tip

~ *Know what you value most in life; this knowledge will help you make decisions based on your priorities. Anxiety comes when the options involved in your decisions conflict with the order of your priorities.*

8

Three Essential Ingredients for a Stress-Free Environment

How many times have you asked, "*Why* did he do that? *Why* did she say that? *Why* does nothing ever work out for me? *Why* didn't I get what I wanted? *Why* does this keep happening in my life?"

"Whyology" is the obsessive need to know why things happen as they do, which results in emotional paralysis, keeping you *stuck*. Why do you need to know why things happen? If you did know, would it make that much difference? Many people will say, "Yes, it would make a difference, because then I would be able to move on and let it go."

The truth is that the letting-go experience has nothing to do with knowing why things happen as they do. In fact, the more you need to know why, the less likely you are to let go and move on.

Unless release this cycle, you will be robbed of your ability to appreciate and enjoy the moment you are living in right now. Think of all the energy that you could use to create in life if you left the practice of keeping vigil to tombstones.

I was diagnosed with stage-3 breast cancer in 2006. I could have remained in a place of denial, anger, worry, doubt, and fear; however, I quickly learned that nothing thrives in a state of *war*.

I also learned that, as with each bump in the road along my treatment journey, I always had the ability to choose how I wanted to respond to the bump. Sometimes I chose anger, denial, and victimization (such as "Why can't my left side just heal up after third-degree burns? It's been *one year* of open wounds."), yet I remember thinking *that* choice didn't feel very good. It sapped my motivation and inner strength, so I didn't stay there too long.

Internal stress comes when you resist what is in life. I remember saying, "I choose love and life no matter what!" Sometimes I would scream it at the top of my lungs. Another version was, "Even though I don't want to right now, because I'm tired and I feel sick, I give God permission to fill me with life and love in spite of myself."

When writing my first book, *Hearing His Whisper...A Journey Through Cancer and Divorce*, I heard a lot of "Thanks, but no thanks" before I found a home for it. Each time I opened a "No-thank-you letter," my internal mantra was: It's not rejection; it's just direction.

When you release your need to know why, an amazing thing starts to happen. You begin to connect with your inner creativity, which helps you find creative solutions to your situation.

You didn't get the promotion you wanted. What are you going to do about it? Rather than dwelling on what you did not get (which, by the way, is mentally exhausting and stressful) and lingering by the closed door, focus on how you want to respond to the situation. If not here, then where?

Seek, ask, and knock

Take action, and part of that action involves *release* and *acceptance* of what is. The clouds of obsessive thinking will clear and the blue skies of inner inspiration will return once again. By doing this, you will unleash your sense of empowerment and release feelings of victimization.

The following are three actions you can take to help you move into the energy that flows from seeking, asking, and knocking in this life. If you do them, you will return to your curious and fascinated energy, which allowed you to crawl or walk into any room when you were a little child without any fear of rejection. (This took place at one point in time before you experienced your first encounter with rejection.)

Remember *you*—before the pain and survival antics kicked in. That was then and this is now. You have many more resources than you had back then, so use them to reconnect to God, who is capable of moving mountains. If not here, then where?

Action #1: Release the need for certain outcomes and responses.

This action item is related directly to your need to know why things happen as they do. Your need to know certain outcomes and responses from the world around you will imprison you. If you need this or that to happen in your life in order to feel good about yourself and excited about your life, then you will rise and fall depending on the events around you. (No, thank you! I tried that and having this need to know doesn't work. Talk about emotionally draining.)

How many moments in your day do you spend waiting, wishing, or hoping that certain things will happen in your life? These thoughts are separate from goals, dreams, and ambitions, which flow from inner creativity and are manifested by being present to the moment you are in and the action you can take in that moment.

What can you do *now* to move in the direction of your goals, dreams, and ambitions? Waiting, wishing, and hoping are all void of the present moment from which action, empowerment, creativity, and inspiration flow. They exist in the future, which, in reality, doesn't exist.

Again, it's okay to want certain outcomes and responses from the world around you. However, when you *need* them in order to feel good about yourself, then you become vulnerable to stress and anxiety. Review the section about attachment and happiness in Chapter 4.

Action #2: Release the inner critic

How much of your day is spent complaining or cutting yourself and others down? Just for fun, carry a note pad with you tomorrow and put down a tally mark for every critical comment or thought of which you are aware. Next to each tally, write "self," "others," or "the world around me."

Once you observe this pattern in your life, you are more apt to choose a different response. It takes practice, so you may have to carry that note pad around for a week or two before you become fully aware of how much the "inner critic" controls your response to life. Nothing stifles creativity and connection faster than the inner critic does. Be very careful what you think, because your body is listening!

For example, water studies conducted in Japan came to my attention during my experience with cancer. The impact of these studies visually inspired me to watch the words I used throughout my treatment and healing.

Our bodies are comprised of 60 percent water.[1] Dr. Masaru Emoto, author of *The Hidden Messages in Water,* discovered that crystals formed in frozen water reveal changes when specific, concentrated thoughts are directed toward them. He found that water from clear springs and water exposed to *loving words* shows brilliant, complex, and colorful snowflake patterns. In contrast, polluted water—water exposed to negative thoughts—forms incomplete, asymmetrical patterns with dull colors.[2] To me, this speaks of the *power of positive words* down to the cellular level.

Taking nothing personally leads to inner peace and the freedom to live and let live. Know this: Anything any human being says or does in your life has nothing to do with you personally, yet you continue to give power to the words people speak to you by allowing their proclamations to define you.

Action #3: Choose positive feedback, encouragement, and affirmation.

When you receive reviews in life from other people, remember that you can choose what is true and what is not true for you. Their words are simply an opinion from their perception of you.

In Chapter 3, we discussed the "writing on your walls" and the power you give to those messages. Anything that any human being says or does has everything to do with the writing on their wall, and the experiences and perceptions they carry within themselves.

Remembering this will help you stay grounded in the truth of who you are the next time you receive what you perceive to be negative feedback. Watch the tone of your voice with yourself and with those around you. Affirm and encourage yourself and others, and observe how positive feedback flows back into your life.

Erase and replace

Starting *today*, condition your system around positive statements. Remember: Your body is listening. Try the Erase and Replace technique created by Gary Craig, the founder of EFT (Emotional Freedom Technique). You can also use the Erase and Replace technique along with the EFT tapping technique found in Chapter 12 to get rid of unwanted negative thinking.

~ *Erase: "I am stressed out."*

~ *Replace: "I have a lot on my plate. I am taking a break."*

~ *Erase: "I'm exhausted."*

~ *Replace: "I am going to rest my body and give it time to refuel."*

~ *Erase: "I can't do that."*

~ *Replace: "I don't know how to do that yet, so I will choose to expand my abilities to learn how."*

~ *Erase: "I hate public speaking."*

~ *Replace: "This is an opportunity to practice my communication skills and remember that I have been public speaking ever since I said my first word in public."*

Take action

One of your greatest places of empowerment lies in your ability to stay awake at the gate. Remain alert as you watch the words that you use to define your life experience.

Life unfolds before you, and you take in the experience of life through your five senses—what you see, feel, hear, touch, taste, and smell. You then organize, code, and define that experience into words. The words with which you choose to define your life experience become a part of your programming. You reference these words as you experience more moments of life.

Negative emotions are a direct result of labeling or coding your life experience as threatening in some way. Life happens, you experience it, and then you label it as good, bad, helpful, or unhelpful. Practice giving yourself permission to experience life rather than defining, controlling, or judging it. As you set up resistance of any kind to the life that is unfolding, you set yourself up for a negative emotion.

All stress is fueled by three main areas: worry, self-doubt, and fear. How do worry, self-doubt, and fear form inside you? They form by the negative label you place on the thoughts you have about your life experience.

Here's an example of this process from my own life experience: I got a phone call that began with, "Lauren, are you sitting down?" It was followed with the news that cancer was found in my body.

This was simply a fact exchange. The doctor called and shared the test results with me, which was information based on tests. Now that I am through the experience of cancer, I can explain this moment as if I am watching a movie from a place of disassociation. I am void of any emotional charge around this past memory.

However, when I was in it, I remember that everything inside me went numb and I could barely feel my legs. As soon as I labeled the information my doctor gave me as threatening to my safety and well-being, my body jumped into the "fight, flight, and freeze" mode of protection. I went into survival mode, which created overwhelming stress in my body.

When my doctors told me that I had advanced cancer in my body, I immediately began to pull from my time line of experience with cancer and the people I knew who had died from it. One of the labels I placed on the diagnosis was, "I might die and I am only 38 years old."

As soon as I reframed that image of myself into a positive one, my entire perspective shifted from negative to positive. I remember praying a prayer of surrender:

Dear God, I surrender all that I am to You. I believe that my natural state of being is created in Your image. I am created in health and strength. I have witnessed my body heal without any conscious effort on my part since the first time I skinned my knee. I give permission to every cell in my body to render itself over to that natural state of healing and restoration. Thank you God for my healing."

After five years of healing and restoration, I still say that prayer.

In addition to the prayer, I use the Swish Pattern, an NLP technique that I learned during my training with the American University of NLP, founded by Steve G. Jones. This practice takes unwanted images or behavior and transforms it into what you want to be or see yourself as being. I want to see myself as healthy, alive, vibrant, and capable of handling any and every situation that comes before me in my life.

Here is a summary of the Swish Pattern technique:

~ *Visualize a large, life-like, colorful image of your desired self-image on a poster. I imagined a bright, powerful, best picture of a healthy, vibrant me in the center of my brain.*

~ *Create another picture of yourself that you wish to remove from your focus. You can apply this to any problem or behavior you wish to remove (for example, smoking, overeating, and drinking). I imagined a picture of myself bald and breastless, weak and defeated.*

~ *Imagine placing the negative picture of yourself in your unwanted condition over the healthy, vibrant picture of yourself, which is the desired image of you that you created. Picture putting a small dot in the center of the unwanted picture and give it the option to open up, similar to a camera shutter. As it opens, it reveals the big, healthy, confident, positive picture of the best you.*

~ *Open your eyes.*

~ *Repeat this process five to six times as you open the negative picture of you, like a camera shutter, revealing the positive image of you, which is vibrant and colorful. Each time you reveal that positive image of you, say the word "swish."*[3]

Any time you receive news that threatens your sense of safety and connection, practice being the watcher of yourself in the midst of it all. Become aware of your body. How does it feel? What images do you see from your past or projected images in the future? What inner dialogue do you hear?

As you allow yourself to observe your reactions to the situation, you will have space to consider and pursue different responses. Talk to the inner dialogue and change your tone of voice. Choose to tune into other moments in your life when you felt out of control and created positive shifts and solutions.

You are capable of choosing your response to any situation. Remember that you are not a victim in this life unless you choose that state of being. God has infused within you the ability to choose your response to any situation in this life. Do not forget your God-given natural state of being to walk on top of water and move mountains.

Use your language to open up possibilities for learning and growth. Words have energy and the power to keep you in unhealthy patterns of response to the world around you. Practice erasing and replacing a few common negative statements that you recorded in your note pad as you are becoming aware of your own "inner critic."

Practice reframing the negative into the positive. Take a piece of paper, fold it in half, and write the following two words on opposite sides of the paper: *erase* and *replace*. Reflect on the statements in your life that keep you stuck in negative thinking, and jot them down in the erase column.

Now, kick your creative thinking into gear, reframe those negative statements into the positive, and write them down under the "replace" column. Weave in words that spark ease and creative thinking (for example, "consider," "explore," "expand," "curious," "fascinated," "effortlessly," "naturally," "unlimited," "opportunity," "experience," and "fun").

For example, when I went through cancer and divorce at the same time, many little thoughts would try to drive my self-esteem ship. Whenever my friends set me up with different guys, I remember glaring at my bald head in the mirror as I got ready for the dates. Those creepy, negative self-talk serpents slithered their way into my thoughts: "Who the heck would want to date a bald and breastless woman?" and "You are going to freak this guy out! The date will be over as soon as you reveal the truth that you are divorced with three kids and are going through advanced cancer. He is going to look like Bugs Bunny running through the wall!" I remember yelling aloud many times, "ENOUGH! God, I give you permission to have your way with my mind, in spite of the negative serpents of self-talk that prevent me from remembering my authentic worth and value."

I wrote down several replacement statements and used them as I got ready for dates:

~ *"God is with me."*

~ *"My authentic beauty is untouchable."*

~ *"I consider tonight an incredible opportunity to expand my awareness of what I am and what I am not."*

~ *"WOW! What an amazing opportunity to practice self-confidence."*

~ *"I no longer rise and fall depending on how the world may judge me or how I judge me."*

~ *"I have a delete button, and I'm not afraid to use it!"*

~ *"My natural beauty flows from the inside out, effortlessly, to all who meet me this evening."*

~ *"I am beautifully and wonderfully created in the image of God."*

~ *"Beauty is my divine, natural state of being."*

~ *"I am untouched by the opinions of other people as I ground my remembrance of who I am."*

~ *"One of the benefits of being bald is that I can style my hair the night before, and it looks the same the next morning!"*

It is important to give yourself permission to feel what you feel in the moment without judgment. Not doing so sets up resistance to what is, and creates internal conflict and stress. Acknowledge where you are with compassion and love.

Then, move into prayer and ask for the grace to remember that you are capable of moving mountains, learning, and growing within every life experience. As you step into recalling your capabilities, reframe your use of language that is in line with that knowing.

Accepting all that you are—including your thoughts—puts you into a state of awareness, which gives you the opportunity to choose your response to life.

Dear God, help me remember that I am infused with love. Move me through this negative place back to inner peace as I remember that I am loved, complete, and capable. Because You live within and through me, all things are possible. Help me to choose words that reflect this prayer in all that I say and respond to in this day.

Grab-and-Go Stress Relief Tips

~ *You cannot always choose the events that unfold in your life. However, you always have the ability to choose how you want to respond to those events.*

~ *Let go of your need to know why things happen as they do. Practice the art of "allowing" in life.*

~ *Your perception makes all the difference in the outcome.*

~ *Look at life as a schoolhouse of opportunity rather than a courthouse of judgment.*

~ *Look at everything in this life as an opportunity for learning. Growth will result in spontaneous creativity and innovation.*

9

Whatever You Choose to Focus on Grows Bigger

Have you ever noticed that, if you start your day off on the wrong side of the bed, events seem to follow the same direction as you go through your day? When you are looking to buy a new dog, house, or car, do you see these things *everywhere*? These are great examples of the power of your attention and focus.

If you focus on the negative (that is, what's *not* working out), you will notice the negative everywhere and in everything until you shift your perception, which is actually a physiological event. You choose the lens through which you see the world.

There is a little piece of your brain called the Reticular Activating System. One of its main jobs is to tune into whatever you choose to focus on. The Reticular Activating System takes information from your conscious mind and transfers it to the subconscious experience. For this exchange to work in your favor, it is essential that you align your sense of self with your goals.

You can program your Reticular Activating System by imagining something and tuning into information aligned with your choice of focus. You form choices by your thoughts; by your choices, you form your life, including your perception of events and situations. *Choose wisely.*

If you focus on what *is* working in your life, you will get more of that quickly. It is *your* choice every minute of every day. What will you focus on?

The practice of presence

Not one minute of your life occurs outside the present moment. Can you live in the future? Can you live in the past? You might say yes, but it's just an illusion in your head.

The truth is that you do not live in the future and in the past, and that is the problem when connecting to your inner inspirations and creativity, which flow from the experience of being present. Present to what? Present to being alive and taking in the wonderment of the gift of life.

Have you ever been in a car and had a "close-call" moment when you could have died? A few years back, my dad and I were going fly fishing and the roads were icy. As I turned the corner, my car kept going right off the side of the mountain and the tires blew off the car. A single tree on the side of the mountain caught the car before it started to roll.

After the car settled and we crawled out, I looked at my dad and said, "We're *alive!* We're ALIVE!"

It's wonderful to remember the elation I felt as a result of the brush with death. How would it be if you could feel that depth of gratitude and joy with each new dawn?

Practice being present to the wonderment of life as it unfolds before you. Reflect when you catch yourself pausing in moving moments. Remember: Whatever you focus on *grows bigger*. Thanks to your Reticular Activating System, if you focus on the beauty and love around you, you will start recognizing more beautiful, loving moments.

Have you ever been in an airplane and felt sure that you were going to crash? Think about what it is you are focused on at the moment. There is no time for "daydreaming." You are acutely present to the situation at hand. As soon as you realize that you are safe, a huge rush of relief comes over you, and you are filled with gratitude for life. Even if your hand is bleeding or you have a bump on your head, it doesn't matter because you think, "I'm ALIVE!"

Try to remember a close-call moment in your life or the life of someone you love, and perspective will return instantly. This will create an environment where you are more likely to choose a positive response to the situation rather than a negative one. Know that whenever you tune into the experience of gratitude and reverence for all of life, you will reconnect with inner peace.

When you are present to the gift of life, you realize in an instant all that is essential before you. The things that you truly value in life will grow bigger, and perspective will seep in between the cracks of your worldly worries.

Living life with a curious and fascinated perspective lends itself to the experience of being present to the life in front of your face. This practice results in *inner peace* and connection to God.

Sometimes you can delay releasing the stress until a later date when you can return a phone call, call a meeting, create a teleseminar, or finish the laundry. (See the stressor/action sheet in Chapter 13.)

Speak in terms of *now*. What can I do *now* to make this, that, or the other thing happen? Having agendas and goals is empowering only if you are present to the moments that lead up to their fulfillment.

God said, "I am," not "I was" or "I will be." Therefore, your greatest source of connection, strength, and creativity occurs in the present moment. We achieve our goals in life one present moment at a time.

Take action

At 38 years old, with three young children, and while going through a divorce, the doctors told me that I had a 50/50 chance of survival. I had no idea about the extent of my survival instinct and my choice for life no matter what I heard. I surrendered everything over to God when I was 17 years old and I used to say this prayer: *Dear God, use my life and my death to bring more love into the world.*

However when death lurked in the shadows I remember falling to the ground and crying out to God: "I take back the death part!"

At the time of the diagnosis, my business was—and still is—teaching people how to maintain inner peace no matter what surrounds them. Here I was, facing two of the top stressors at the same time: cancer and divorce. In less than two years, I experienced a divorce, a double mastectomy, 16 chemotherapy treatments, an additional year of chemo, six weeks of daily radiation, 12 surgeries due to third-degree burns from the radiation/chemo combination (they had to graft my back onto my front), and a methicillin-resistant staphylococcus aureus (MRSA) staph infection that almost took my life. I say this without any sense of victimization because this was truly a schoolhouse of opportunity to practice and apply what I had been teaching and learning about for 20 years.

I remember standing in the shower, bald and breastless, surveying the scars on my chest where my breasts used to be as I said aloud, "Wow! I am earning my PhD in suffering, which will give me the ability to connect to the hearts of humanity through vulnerability."

When you remember that you have the God-given ability to shift your perception of any situation that unfolds before you, the portal of healing and opportunity for growth opens up right before your eyes. After speaking engagements, people will approach me and share pieces from their "dark night of the soul" experiences.

Oftentimes, they will start out by saying, "Well, this is nothing compared to what *you* have been through."

I respond by reminding them of the following things:

~ *Be present to the lessons and learning opportunities in the midst of your perceived threatening situation. Don't miss the invitation to move beyond your limitations.*

~ *No two human hearts beat the same. Comparisons only occur when people forget their worth, uniqueness, and capability.*

~ *Use your unique challenge to reconnect to what you value most in this life. When you begin to see what is nonessential and essential in light of this choice, inner peace will return.*

Be a seeker of rainbows, no matter what surrounds you, and you will see them appear in the most unlikely situations. Program your Reticular Activating System (RAS) to tune into the positive in your life and what *is* working out for you. I made the choice for God, life, and love—no matter what surrounded me. For the first time in five years, I have stopped all medication related to the cancer.

Here is one of my daily mantras:

Even though I am not perfect, I am willing to love and accept myself anyway. To accept me, just as I am, with or without hair, a successful marriage, a strong body, or breasts was a process and an invitation to myself as connected to God.

I love my ability to choose God, life, and love, no matter what surrounds me, along with my choice to give myself permission to begin again. I appreciate every breath, heartbeat, and opportunity to grow in the ways of love with the gift of each new dawn.

Choose one day, and focus on what is working for you in *that* day—all day. At the end of your day, write down what you felt inside and how that day was different as a result of your choice to focus on, recognize, appreciate, and acknowledge all that *is* working out for you in life.

When I was going through the cancer experience, the practice of releasing parts of my physical appearance was very powerful. When I shifted my focus from what I was losing to what I had going for me, my entire perception of life shifted to the positive. I could see, hear, smell, walk, speak, share, receive, give, and love.

From that perspective, I lacked nothing in my day.

Grab-and-Go Stress Relief Tips

~ *Whatever you focus on in your life will grow bigger quickly.*

~ *Not one minute of your life occurs outside of the present moment unfolding in front of your face. Get out of your imagined future and your "if only" and "whyology" matrix of your past.*

~ *Practice presence now. When your focus is on living life now, you will find that doubt, fear, and scarcity cease to exist.*

10

Making the Shift

No one is capable of making you upset without your consent.
—Wayne Dyer

Feelings of being overcome by life's challenges flow directly from the perception that you are not okay and cannot handle what is before you. As these feelings come up in your day, a simple shift in your focus can help guide you out of the mental freeze. Perhaps try something like this:

I just don't know how, yet I have confidence that I will find a way. I have found a way many times in the past. I choose to open myself up to God's strength and wisdom within me to move through this. I acknowledge that I am feeling overwhelmed and scared that I will not be able to handle this. I choose to love and accept all that I am in the midst of this self-doubt. I am willing to consider that I am forgetting the times in my life when I felt this way and moved through it easily. I choose to remember my God-given strength and ability to overcome.

Taking action with confidence in your ability to handle new situations will lead you into the experience of conquering perceived threats in life rather than being overcome by them. Remember: *You are okay all the time.* You simply forget this in the midst of the sensory overload, which occurs in your brain when the tsunamis of life wash over you.

Connect with your body through being self-aware, breathing deeply, placing your hand on your heart, and tuning into your ability to see and hear the life in front of your face. This will help you drop out of your head where you feel attacked. You may not still be in the physical jungle; however, the jungle still exists in your head. Your empowerment returns when you remember that you don't have to live there anymore.

From fear to love

Think of the many times that you have heard about this everyday choice in life: "I can live in fear *or* I can live by love." Again, when you allow yourself to feel what you feel without judgment, the outcome is very powerful.

When fear comes up, allow love to come with it, along with a compassionate acknowledgment of your emotional state:

I am aware that I am feeling this fear. I am afraid that I won't be accepted. I am afraid that I won't love myself if this event does not occur the way I want it to. I am afraid that I will let others down. I am unworthy and unloved. Even though I feel this way right now, I am willing to remember how quickly I have moved through emotions like this in the past. I am willing to love and accept myself. I am willing to remember my ability to move through emotional experiences like this in life.

Fear hits you at times when you least expect it. When this happens, you are often connecting to one of your past holographs, which has been uploaded into your system.

For example, you are 10 years old and swimming in a pool, and your friends think it's funny to hold you under the water. In an instant, you connect water with fear, which can lead to a phobia. Another example is that you are in college, giving a presentation, and a few people in the back are laughing among themselves. You make the connection between public speaking and fear of rejection.

These are isolated events that, in and of themselves, have no power over you unless you define yourself and your sense of safety by them. A powerful shift statement can help separate your current situation from past fears:

That was then and this is now. I am safe now. I have many available resources of which I am more aware today than I was back then. I choose to release the hold this fear has on me in my life.

The common fear of "What will other people think of me?" was discussed earlier (see Chapter 2). The reason that this is a fear for you is because you give power to the words other people speak to you. You give them the power to define you.

Many of you have had negative responses growing up when you shared your opinions; as a result, you felt disempowered, ridiculed, invalidated, and shut down. You also learned quickly how to protect yourself from those negative feelings:

If I don't talk, and don't share my opinions, insights, and inspirations, then I won't risk feeling invalidated and disempowered.

Talk about a block to effective communication and public speaking. Many of the conflicts you experience communicating with others around you flow from this type of "protection mode." Tune into a specific event in your life when you felt ridiculed or disempowered and write it down. This will help you make the shift into love.

Even though I felt disempowered and ridiculed when this happened, I am willing to consider that I am safe now. That was then and this is now. I am willing to believe that what I have to share with the world holds value, uniqueness, and creativity.

The previous statement is an example of how to love yourself well in life. As you know, how you treat others around you flows directly from how you treat yourself. Your ability to love and value others in this life flows directly from your ability to love and value yourself. As Jesus said in Mark 12:31, "Love your neighbor as yourself." Who you are is separate from the opinions of other people.

I grew up with this positive message: "You only feel inferior by your own consent."

You are not a victim here. Take back your ability to define you.

It's not rejection—it's just direction

Soul retrieval exercise

Make a list of all the people in your life to whom you have given permission to define you in some way. You can use the gift of your imagination to access the memory of the people to whom you gave away your power of identity along your journey.

Close your eyes, take a few relaxed, deep breaths, and imagine floating above your time line from a place of quick, easy observation. Pause during the moments that grab your attention, and observe the people involved during these moments that stand out. Perhaps a coach continued to point out your weaknesses, a teacher was indifferent to your personal successes in class, or someone verbally or physically abused you. Give yourself the time to reflect, and gather this list of people who played a negative role, from your perception, in the formation of your identity.

Review your list and, after each name, say the following words:

I gave you the power to define me, and today I take it back with love and compassion. I understand that, when I gave you the power to define me, I was doing the best I could do in light of my awareness of the available resources at that moment in time. That was then and this is now.

As I mentioned earlier in Chapter 8, this mantra came to me when I was trying to find a publisher for my first book, *Hearing His Whisper...A Journey Through Cancer and Divorce.*

You have the ability to choose your response to any and every situation that unfolds before you in your life. You are not a victim unless you choose to be one. Remember that victimization leads to emotional paralysis and the inability to come up with creative solutions.

Until you take *full* responsibility for your life—and I mean *everything* in your life—you will stay stuck. However, as soon as you do take full responsibility for your life, the skies will open before you. The energy you spent playing the victim in life can now be used to create, reframe, connect, inspire, and live out a purpose-filled life.

"I am enough, just as I am."

Many of you go back and forth all day saying, "I can do this...no, I can't...yes, I can...no, I can't." This banter happens between your true self (your soul) and your false self (your perception of *you* based on the "writing on your wall" and false beliefs).

Your soul knows that it is complete, capable, and creative—lacking nothing at any time for overcoming perceived challenges in life. This is "deathbed" wisdom, which can change your entire perspective if you start believing that you are okay and safe in this world, just as you are.

Your soul has a humble awareness, filled with gratitude and appreciation for the breath of life and all that comes with it. All of your feelings of lack and scarcity flow from two thoughts: "I am unlovable" and "I am unworthy." When you infuse your awareness of your emotional state with love and compassion, peace returns. With that in mind, try this sentence: "Even though I feel (insert feeling), I am willing to love and accept myself anyway."

Your "false self" exhausts itself by analyzing, comparing, and judging. It often says statements like "I'm not safe. I'm not loved or accepted. The world is out to get me. I am unappreciated."

Your "false self" spends its day in an anxious state, striving to prove to the world that it is worthy of love and acceptance. It misses the wonderment and creativity that flow from being present to the soul, remembering that your experience of being loved is omnipresent.

God's love for you is limitless and constant. No thing or experience on Earth can separate you from the love of God. When you remember this, you will experience the peace that passes all human understanding.

When you believe yourself to be loved and accepted, just as you are, all of your antics in striving to prove that you are enough will disappear. You will connect to your God-given creativity, along with the confidence and motivation to *go for it* in this life!

You will step into the wondering of an unknown author, who said, "What would you dare to do if you knew you could not fail?"

Love transforms the human heart; judgments of yourself and other people imprison it. This definition of judgment refers to criticism and censorship. Stop the insanity of this kind of judgment. You judge other people because you feel that you are not enough, or you are threatened that someone else may have the power to compromise your beliefs or take something away from you.

Judgment serves no one in this world and ends up hardening your beautiful heart and cutting it off from explosive creativity and innovation along with life-giving connection. Positive connection flows from an open mind and a compassionate heart. As soon as you make a judgment of another human being, you stop learning.

Take action

Pick a day this week and call it "No Judgment Day." See how long you can go without criticizing or condemning yourself and those around you.

This practice has great rewards. You will gain insight into the meaning behind people's words and behavior, and your heart will open to compassion and love. As you encounter a human being acting out his or her pain, and remember that you are worthy and loved from within, you will respond with grace: "Perhaps this person is forgetting how loved and valuable he or she is today."

You will be free from your antics, which flow from taking personally everything that another human being says or does. Imagine the amount of freed-up creative space you would have within your mind if you released all judgments toward yourself and people around you. This is an invitation for you to practice experiencing life rather than making judgments about your life experiences.

Be aware of your eye movements during the day, including how often you look down and particularly to the left. Often, when your eyes drift downward to the left, you are accessing your inner dialogue. If the dialogue is positive, then the emotional state will follow; however, if your inner dialogue is predominantly negative, then negative emotions will remain.

When I am working with clients one on one, I watch their eye movements. I have noticed consistently that, when a client is in an emotionally negative downward spiral, their eyes will drift down to the left. I will often catch them and encourage them to look up to the right, which enables them to access the part of their brain where they can create a new, positive visual of the situation at hand.

In the Old Testament, there are many references to the experience of lifting your eyes to the heavens in order to access comfort and help. Physiologically speaking, God has given us the ability to create new, positive images by looking up—in most cases to the right.

Create a visual of acceptance and love for yourself and for those around you. By nature, people gravitate toward that which is familiar. Many of my clients have expressed an uncomfortable feeling as they consciously look up to the right to create positive visual images toward themselves and others.

I encourage you to practice hanging out in that creative zone. Because the inner dialogue for a majority of human beings is negative, you can use this knowledge to fuel your desire to create positive, loving responses to yourself and to other people. Love evokes more love. When you judge yourself or anyone around you, you are putting yourself in a position of determining your worth or their worth.

This week, give yourself permission to experience this statement: "I am enough, just as I am." How would your acceptance of knowing that God is with you, and loves you just as you are, free you from placing judgment on other people? You can only give out what you allow yourself to experience within your own emotional capacity to feel loved and accepted.

One of my favorite passages in the Bible is in John 8:1–11. The teachers of the Law and the Pharisees throw a woman caught in the act of adultery in front of Jesus, proclaiming that, in the Law of Moses, women caught in this act must be stoned to death.

How many times in your life have you thrown yourself or another person in front of your inner law of judgment? Jesus' response to these accusers is applicable today when it comes to casting instant perspective on the antics of judgment in our own lives.

As a practicing Jew, Jesus could have easily jumped on the Law of Moses bandwagon, yet He invites His onlookers to step into an expansive, new way of thinking and respond to the self-imposed limitations set in place each time a human being crawls into the judgment seat. Instead, He brilliantly responds with a thought-provoking, soul-examining, and life-transforming statement in John 8:7: "If any one of you is without sin, let him be the first to throw a stone at her."

The older onlookers were the first to drop their stones, perhaps because they had enough life experience to remember the depth from which they had been saved—maybe more than once—as their need to own, control, and possess evoked an unloving, unkind response to those around them throughout their lifetime.

I invite you to enter into "No Judgment Day" with all of your heart, mind, soul, and strength as you explore and discover a newfound freedom in the experience of loving and being loved in this world—without conditions and restrictions.

Grab-and-Go Stress Relief Tips

~ *You can't always choose what unfolds before you in life, yet you can choose your response to the situation, which makes all of the difference in the outcome.*

~ *People gravitate toward that which is familiar. Give yourself permission to feel safe while moving into the unfamiliar, especially when the unfamiliar is filled with opportunity for learning and growth in the ways of loving on Earth: God, yourself, and others.*

~ *You will experience positive and negative perceptions of life throughout your day. When you respond to both with awareness, infused with love and compassion, your peace will return. Your feelings of lack and scarcity flow from your feelings of being unlovable and unworthy. Acknowledge when you are in this place, and choose to recover forgotten pieces of information from your life experience that guide you back to the experience of love and acceptance.*

11

A Proverb That Can Save Your Life

Throughout the experience of cancer and divorce, I participated in cognitive psychology therapy as well as energy psychology sessions. I was amazed at the powerful and quick transformations I experienced around deep emotional pain using energy psychotherapy modalities such as EFT and NLP. According to Susan Heitler, PhD, a clinical psychologist in Denver, "Energy psychotherapies are to traditional psychotherapy as the alternative physical therapies like acupuncture are to medical treatment. We do not really know how or why they work, but the potency of their healing impacts are [sic] clearly evident."[1]

NLP explores six logical levels for personal transformation:

Spirit -> Identity -> Beliefs -> Capabilities -> Behavior -> Environment

Imagine an upside-down pyramid format, with the spirit logical level at the top and the environment level at the bottom, and a big funnel flowing down from the top (spirit) to the bottom (environment).

If you create a positive shift in your spirituality, then each level below the spirit will experience change. Expanding your spirituality in a positive direction is the highest level of personal transformation. The choice to make a positive shift at the level of your soul creates a domino effect, inspiring and transforming your identity, beliefs, capabilities, behavior, and environment. Every logical level in the pyramid will affect itself and every level underneath it.

You are a spiritual person, first and foremost, living in a physical world. Your capabilities and beliefs fall between your identity and behaviors. Your environment is where your behavior happens. Your behavior is what you do, think, and say.

Many people will come to me as a Master NLP Practitioner, seeking to change their behavior (stop smoking, get in shape, decrease daily stress, create positive connections at work/home, increase their confidence, release fears/phobias, and stop compulsive behaviors). I will address the behavior and shift the experiences in their day-to-day environment; however, when the client is willing, I will invite them to explore the opportunities to make a change to a higher level, considering that many people's higher-level identity is wrapped up in their behavior.

The behaviors you manifest in your life flow from the highest logical level of your spirituality and identity. When you make a shift to a higher level from the highest logical level, your spirituality and your environment will shift accordingly. With that in mind, the rest of this chapter will focus on your spirituality.

Simply put, your soul connection with God drives the rest of your ship in life. When you are disconnected from a relationship with God—your highest source of guidance, wisdom, and love—you begin to fragment the rest of your inverted pyramid:

~ **Your Spirit:** *The side of you as a spiritual creature, and your purpose in life.*

~ **Your Identity:** *Who you are specifically.*

~ **Your Beliefs:** *What you believe and value in life.*

~ **Your Capabilities:** *Your gifts and talents, and what you are capable of doing or accomplishing.*

~ **Your Behavior:** *What you think, say, and do.*

~ **Your Environment:** *Where what you do actually happens.*

When you have a fragmented pyramid, you begin to feel unsafe in certain realms of your life relationships, personal growth, sense of purpose, drive, and motivation. Two basic human needs are safety and connection. When these start to slip in your life, your stress hormones begin to have their way with you.

In 2 Peter 1:19, "A man is enslaved to whatever has mastered him." As you reflect on your own relationship with the world, what has mastered you in your life? Is it your environment? Opinions and reactions of other people? The need to be seen, acknowledged, and recognized? Is it your behavior? My clients, who are seeking freedom from compulsive behavior, will often say, "I just can't help myself." This reveals a type of personal enslavement due to allowing some food, substance, situation, or person to master them over time, which in some cases results in a biological addiction.

The stress hormone is linked directly to your emotional state of mind and heart. Extended emotional stress often leads to personal enslavement, which usually walks hand in hand with unhealthy outlets. The key to freedom in situations like this lies in your ability to accept where you are, accompanied by a desire for positive personal transformation and a choice to take a step in that direction.

As you explore and expand your soul connection with God, the chains that hold you back from personal excellence and empowerment will begin to lose their grip on you. As you resurrect your remembrance of the divine power that courses through your being, an exhilarating experience of detachment begins to emerge, along with peace and wisdom that passes all human understanding. With increased frequency, you will begin to experience moments that are free from your need to own, control, possess, analyze, and conclude, along with your need to know why things happen as they do and how things will turn out. You will begin to gravitate toward the experience of presence. Being here now will begin to take on a light-hearted playfulness toward the moment of life in front of your face.

As you draw near to God at the beginning of each day and throughout your day, your authentic God-given nature begins to emerge on the front lines of your life. You are reminded of your expansive value, worth, and purpose. You will no longer rise and fall depending on how the world judges you. The stress you have experienced resulting from endless comparisons, jealousies, and moments of envy will no longer enslave you. Once again, you will gain inner freedom to be you, as you remember yourself as loved completely, just as you are, by the God of the universe.

As I went through the divorce and two years of treatment for stage-3 breast cancer, two verses from the bible were posted by my bedside. They reminded me that my God-given natural state of being is health and restoration, flowing from my soul into all other aspects of my life, and equipping me with the strength needed to rise above and move through any stressor that unfolds before me:

Do you not know? Have you not heard? The Lord is the everlasting God, the creator of the ends of the earth. He will not grow tired or weary, and his understanding no one can fathom. He gives strength to the weary and increases the power of the weak. Even youths grow tired and weary, and young men stumble and fall; but those who hope in the Lord will renew their strength. They will soar on wings like eagles; they will run and not grow weary, they will walk and not faint. (Isaiah 40:28–31)

The next verses reminded me of my main source for wisdom in the midst of my personal challenges through two of life's top stressors at the same time:

Who is wise and understanding among you: Let him show it by his good life, by deeds done in humility that comes from wisdom. But if you harbor bitter envy and selfish ambition in your hearts, do not boast about it or deny the truth. Such "wisdom" does not come down from heaven but is earthly, unspiritual, of the devil. For where you have envy and selfish ambition, there you find disorder and every evil practice. But the wisdom that comes down from heaven is first of all pure; then peace-loving, considerate, submissive, full of mercy and good fruit, impartial and sincere. Peacemakers who sow in peace raise a harvest of righteousness. (James 3:13–18)

Step into and explore your own spirituality on a daily basis—the highest logical level that holds in itself the power to expand and strengthen your identity, beliefs, capabilities, behavior, and environment for your highest good and the good of those around you.

Take action

My first book, *Hearing His Whisper,* contains my personal conversations with Jesus before, during, and after the experience of cancer. The conversations began approximately five years prior to the divorce and cancer.

I have been studying history's greatest spiritual teachers since I was a teenager. This is a common belief that emerged before me as I read hundreds of spiritual writings. When a person takes the time to create stillness before God through silence, simple conversation, and meditation, the whisper of God's voice begins to emerge, speaking very clear messages of love, guidance, wisdom, and profound inner peace to the one who sits, asks, seeks, and listens.

I once heard Mother Teresa speak in person. She said that communion with God is much like a fish in water. This is true. No matter where the fish swims, it is surrounded constantly by the presence of water—in, through, and around the fish. When the fish jumps out of the water, it realizes that the water is its life force. When it wiggles its way back into the water, the fish never takes the water for granted again.

Take time this week to pick out a good spiritual read that nourishes your soul and expands your relationship and connection with God. Carve out anywhere from five to 20 minutes of your day and sit still, seek, speak, and feel the presence of God within and around you.

You may say, "I never hear the voice of God speaking to me when I ask questions."

When I began to seek out the experience of hearing God's voice in my life, I would sit before Him, lay my questions out, and then listen. I heard the silence, which produced an unexpected peace inside my body. I then began to respond to my questions the way I thought God would respond. Perhaps I was pulling from years of reading and studying the scriptures and from the writings of history's great spiritual mystics to produce answers to my questions. Either way, I believe it opened the portal to my own encounter with the voice of God. I began to say the prayer of Samuel, which is found in the Old Testament (1 Samuel 3:9), when Eli instructed Samuel to pray a simple prayer ("Speak Lord, your servant is listening") after Eli realized it was God who was speaking to Samuel.

As the days and weeks passed, and I continued to show up every day, seeking to hear God speak, I remember thinking, "Why not me?" Then, the voice of God became clearer and more specific to my situations and wonderings. My peace, as well as my ability to surrender all to God increased. Having full confidence, like a fish in water, He sustains my life on all logical levels.

The choice to move from your soul into the world creates a place of strength and peace within, which is free from common worldly stressors and threats. When your heart is at peace with your God, your body and your life experiences will respond accordingly.

Honor your highest logical level: your spirituality. Begin this week by giving yourself the gift of time. Expand awareness of your spiritual connection with God. The world screams and God whispers. Take the time to hear His whisper.

Grab-and-Go Stress Relief Tips

~ *Stress acts as a fertilizer to cancer cells.*[2]

~ *"A heart at peace gives life to the body but envy rots the bones" (Proverbs 14:30).*

~ *Make your spirituality top priority and inspire your entire life experience.*

~ *Choose your thoughts and contemplations wisely. Your body is listening!*

12

Getting Your Energy Behind the Shift: Emotional Freedom Techniques

Simply put, EFT is acupuncture without the needles (that is, emotional acupuncture). Founded by engineer Gary Craig, whose therapy training includes NLP and Thought Field Therapy, EFT is a simple technique that uses light tapping on your body to realign the body's energy system gently, without the discomfort of needles.

Your energy system freezes when something in life triggers an emotional response within you. The body actually experiences a *zzzzzt* energy disconnect in the face of a distressing memory or event, and you may go into a state of emotional paralysis.

EFT gets the energy moving again, which enables you to reconnect with God, others, and yourself in spite of the anxiety and pain. This reconnect leads to quick reframing opportunities and, therefore, quick emotional healing takes place. Unlike other energy healing methods, EFT incorporates an emotional element to the healing process, addressing unresolved emotional issues as a contributing cause of physical disease, psychological dysfunction, and personal performance limits.

Much of your pain and anxiety is a direct result from not accepting and loving yourself, just as you are. As soon as you verbalize your willingness to love and accept yourself completely—in spite of all the trauma, hardship, and pain you have experienced—a positive message is sent to the cellular level, releasing tension in your body. This creates a positive inner environment for healing to take place.

As a result of this release method, I have experienced very few physical and emotional side effects to the cancer treatments during the past five years. I use this method every day to release the negative charge in my body in response to perceived threats in life.

Because I feel instant relief, this method has become my favorite stress relief tool. Through the past seven years, I have empowered thousands of people with the ability to use this technique in their daily lives and have witnessed profound physical and emotional results.

Healing at your fingertips

EFT is not connected to any New Age philosophy or spiritual or religious practice. This mechanical technique is similar to physical therapy, which helps the body reconnect after an experience of disconnect from emotional blocks and pain.

Negative emotions cause a disruption in your body's flow at the energy points. Your body then becomes unbalanced, which results in both physical and emotional stress. Similar to the benefits of using electroencephalography (EEG) and an electrocardiogram (EKG) to monitor energy connections in our brain and heart, EFT monitors our inner energy connections that are disrupted because of emotional pain and false beliefs, and offers a way to reconnect.

EFT helps rewire your energetic system, which is in a "frozen" state because of an emotional or physical event. Imagine a television set that is experiencing static. The TV is in a frozen state because there is some kind of confusion in its wiring or connection. As soon as you rewire or reconnect it, the clarity of the picture returns.

As soon as you restore balance to your system using this tapping technique, you return to a state of inner balance. Therefore, you are no longer upset when faced with the same situation that upset you earlier. I believe this technique is a beautiful gift from God, working with how you are woven together and how your body responds to the environment around you. Perhaps the method should be included in a handbook at birth entitled *How to Be a Human Being 101*. Imagine how helpful that would have been after you entered the world!

Consider what happens when people have heart attacks. In an attempt to save a life, an electric current is sent through the body to start the heart. Do you remember feeling a shock after walking across a carpet with fuzzy socks? (I used to have "shock wars" with my brothers and sister growing up.)

An electrical circuit runs through your body and sends messages to your brain, which controls all of your functions, both emotional and physical. These centers or energy points, called "meridians," are found in different places along the electrical circuit of your body.

As you tune into your distressing event, memory, or physical pain (being as specific as possible), while tapping with your fingertips on the different meridians, you are able to collapse the negative charge that you hold around the physical or emotional pain.

Be specific and consistent

Before you start tapping, check in with your emotional or physical pain and rate it on a scale from one to 10: My emotional or physical pain rate is:

Choose a setup statement, which describes with ruthless honesty what you feel and your distressing event. Avoid global statements like "Even though I'm stressed out," or "Even though I have low self-esteem." The more specific you can be, the better the results.

Be as specific as you can with your wording. Here are four setup statement examples:

1. *"Even though I'm really ticked off that my boss told me today that I was incompetent, I am willing to love and accept myself, just as I am."*
2. *"Even though I have a huge headache that is throbbing behind my eyes, I am willing to love and accept myself anyway."*
3. *"Even though I feel this small pain the size of a golf ball in my upper right shoulder...."*
4. *"Even though I felt rejected when Lauren said this to me and I had a hard time breathing...."*

Repeat your setup statement *three times* while tapping the side of your hand (karate chop point) or rubbing the sore spots located 2 inches down from the U-shaped dip in your neck and 3 inches over on each side:

1. *"Even though:*
   I am willing to love and accept myself, just as I am."
2. *"Even though:*
   I am willing to love and accept myself, just as I am."
3. *"Even though:*
   I am willing to love and accept myself, just as I am."

Tune in emotionally to the issue and connect with your emotional response as much as possible. Use the gift of your imagination to remember all that you felt during the distressing memory or moment. Use visualization to imagine yourself in the situation that caused you the anxiety, or focus on your physical pain.

Once you are tuned into your issue, begin tapping on the outer soft side of your hand (the karate chop point) or rub the sore spots (located 2 inches down from the U-shaped dip in your neck and 3 inches over on each side).

Tap on the issue at hand as soon as possible. The quicker you can get your energy moving around the *zzzzzt* disconnect in your body, the better.

After repeating your setup statement three times, you are ready to move through a sequence of points while stating a reminder phrase that links you to your setup statement.

Use the example I previously mentioned: "Even though I have a huge headache that is throbbing behind my eyes, I am willing to love and accept myself anyway."

Then, take a one- or two-word reminder phrase, such as "this headache," and, using your fingertips, lightly tap five to seven times on the following points as you say your reminder phrase one time at each point. You can do both hands tapping on both sides at the same time, one side at a time, or a combination. For instance, I prefer to use both hands tapping on the two eyebrow points, outside of the eyes, and top of the cheek bone, and then use one hand to tap on the point under the nose, under the lip, collar bone, and so on.

EFT sequence tapping points

Here is a description and the sequence of meridian points, which are near the surface of the body and easy to access. Tap these after you say the setup statement three times:

~ *The beginning of the eyebrows, just above and to the side of the nose.*

~ *The outside of your eye socket bone, between your eyes and your temples.*

~ *Under your eyes on the top of the cheekbone, about 1 inch below your pupil.*

~ *Under your nose, between your upper lip and the bottom of your nose.*

~ *Halfway between your chin and the bottom of your lower lip.*

~ *1 inch down and 1 inch over from the bottom of the U-shaped dip on your collarbone at the base of your throat.*

~ *Under your arm for men and along the bra strap line for women. (Use your four fingers to tap on this point under the arm.)*

~ *The liver point about 1 inch down from the nipple for men and right under the breast for women.*

~ *The outside edge of your thumb at a point right next to the thumbnail.*

~ *The outside edge of your index finger at the nail (facing your thumb).*

~ *The side of your middle finger at the point by the nail (the side closest to your thumb).*

~ *The inside of the baby finger (the side closest to your thumb).*

~ *The top of the head.*

~ *The karate chop point on the soft side of your hand (End with this.)*

I will often leave out the finger points when I tap and get the same results. I add them if I feel stuck.

After you have said your setup statement three times, and tapped a round of the sequence points while stating the reminder phrase, check to see how high your pain is (emotional or physical) on the scale from one to 10. Sometimes, the number will get higher before it drops.

Keep tapping the sequence of points while saying,

"...this remaining (insert your reminder phrase)."

Keep checking in and tapping until you reach 0.

Don't stress out about memorizing these points. If you take your time and learn a few each day, soon you will be tapping in your sleep.

As mentioned previously, before you begin to tap, it's helpful to rate your stressful situation or physical pain on a scale from one to 10. Then, tap for a while and try to tune back into your issue to see if the number drops down on the scale. If you keep tapping until you get down to 0, it is unlikely that a specific aspect of your painful memory or event will return.

We all have tabletop issues, such as low self-esteem and phobias, which can have many aspects. For example, you may have a fear of speaking in public or experience claustrophobia, which could be connected to a painful memory. Perhaps, as a child, you accidentally locked yourself in a closet and could not get out. You felt trapped, unheard, and overlooked; you couldn't breathe and felt powerless.

Each of these aspects associated with the trauma of being locked in a closet defines your fear of closed spaces, yet each one must be dealt with specifically. Tap on all of them:

1. *"Even though I felt trapped in that closet and couldn't get out, I am willing to love and accept myself anyway."*

2. *"Even though I couldn't breathe and thought I was going to die, I am willing to love and accept myself."*

Each aspect must be released (that is, tapped on until you reach 0) in order for the issue to lose its negative effect on you; however, there are many times when your aspects are linked together. Therefore, when you collapse one, you collapse them all—"Hey, it's no big deal! Why did that upset me so much? I'm over it!"—you replace the anxiety instantly and you suddenly feel lighter.

EFT is a very forgiving technique, so you don't have to perfect it. As soon as you recognize that *zzzzt* disconnect in your body because of a physical or emotional pain, start tapping.

One time, I was on a plane and I thought we were going down. I was stressed out, so I started to tap. In my peripheral vision, I noticed the head of the man sitting next to me slowly turn toward me as I was tapping. I just kept going because I wanted to release the anxiety in my body, which I knew was coming.

Very compassionately, this man asked me if I had some nervous disorder and I started to laugh. I can't tell you how many times I have been asked questions like that or gotten crazy looks from people next to me. I just smile and say, "This looks a bit crazy, but it works!"

I believe that EFT is a brilliant revelation into the wisdom of how God's energy moves through me. I use this technique to keep that flow of energy moving through my being, thus minimizing the experience of emotional and physical blocks that prevent me from embracing the joy of the present moment.

I tap on and off, all day long. Whenever I feel that *zzzzt* disconnect in my system because of an inner trigger, I begin to move my energy around that disconnected feeling. I have learned from my own experience that the more I keep my energy moving, the less likely I am to experience the "deer in the headlights" response to events unfolding around me.

As mentioned in Chapter 3, you learn your beliefs and then guard them. I will often use the following mantra as I tap on the energy points to release the stress caused around this belief:

In order to be accepted, and accept myself, I do not need to be perfect. Even though I think I need to be perfect in order to receive love and acceptance, I am willing to love and accept myself anyway, and I choose to remember that I am created in God's image beautifully and wonderfully. I choose to be open to the beautiful moments of God's love for me today and freely share that love with those around me.

Combining your EFT statements with Dr. Patricia Carrington's "Choices Method"[1] is very powerful because you end with a positive statement. Dr. Pat's method weaves into the positive statements throughout the tapping and recommends that you address the negative emotional or physical charge for one complete tapping round, and then alternate saying the "issue" reminder statement and your positive choice, and end with one complete tapping round on the meridian points saying your positive statement only. For example, if you have a headache, your first setup statement and tapping round would focus on the actual headache. The second round would involve alternating statements between the headache and your positive choice:

"This number 10 headache...I choose to relax all blood vessels and release restriction...the pounding headache...I give my body permission to return to a state of inner peace

and relief...this head pressure...I choose inner release and calm throughout my entire brain."

Then the third round would consist your positive choice statement only as you tap through all of the meridian points:

"Inner calm...relaxed thinking...I choose to surprise myself at how easy I am able to release ALL pressure in my head... release and peace...I've had a calm, comfortable brain in the past and I believe I can have it in the present."

It is important to ignite as much emotion behind your statements of positive choice to help shift your perception and biological response to emotional tension in the body.

After your setup statement, add your positive choice at the end:

"Even though:
I am willing to love and accept myself, just as I am, and I choose:

Be specific, creative, and expressive when you state your choice.

Be persistent. If you do not feel the anxiety clear up around a specific memory or event, keep looking for other aspects that may be linked to the experience. Tap on all of them individually until you get them down to 0.

Take action

Pick a situation that happened today and caused you anxiety. Rate your pain on a scale from one to 10. Be very specific with your setup statement:

"Even though:
I am willing to deeply and completely love and accept myself, and I choose:

Tap on all of the points described earlier while you say a reminder phrase that is linked to your setup statement. Check in with your pain and continue tapping on the sequence of points, saying:

"This remaining (use your reminder phrase)."

You don't have to repeat the setup statement unless you switch the aspect on which you are tapping. You can use EFT on all of the statements worthy of reflection contained within this book.

Being persistent and specific when tuning into the issue that is causing you "dis-ease" in your body (physically or emotionally) is the key to your success with EFT.

The following are a few examples of the words I used when using the EFT technique to release the negative charge from my past programming that no longer served me:

"When I grew up in Long Island, New York, there was a lot of emphasis on hair (for example, how you styled your hair, how big you got your hair to be, and how long your hair held a style on humid days). This emphasis reinforced a program in the matrix of my self-image, which said: If my hair looks good, I feel good about myself."

Then, when I stood before myself, completely bald 14 days after my first chemo treatment at 38 years old, my self-confidence took a negative hit and my inner dialogue went something like this: "As a woman, if I don't have hair, then I'm not attractive and I don't feel good about myself."

One day, at the checkout counter at the grocery store, I noticed how much emphasis is placed on hair and breasts on the covers of magazines. As I watched TV, every ad for clothes, make-up, and hair products screamed at me as if to say, "Your beauty and identity as a woman in society are directly connected to your hair, breasts, and eyelashes."

My internal dialogue responded by concluding: "If I don't have hair and breasts, and eyebrows and eyelashes, then my experience as a beautiful woman no longer exists."

What a wonderful discovery! I never realized how much I had farmed out my identity as a woman to my hair and breasts. This was an invitation to remember that I am not my hair, my breasts, a statistic, the damage in my body, or any possible side effects to medication.

Here are four specific topics on which I used the EFT technique and experienced profound results throughout my journey with cancer:

1. *EFT setup statement: "Even though I lost all of my hair, I deeply and profoundly love and accept all of me, including my bald head!"*

Reminder phrases I used as I tapped on the EFT Sequence of Tapping Points:

~ *Bald.*

~ *My baldness.*

~ *No hair.*

~ *Completely bald.*

~ *Not even a shadow.*

~ *Am I a man or woman?*

~ *Casper the Ghost, Star Wars, Alien?*

I follow each EFT tapping round with a positive choice round:[2]

~ *I choose to come up with creative ways to celebrate my baldness.*

~ *I give myself permission to be right where I am.*

~ *I choose to feel beautiful.*

~ *I choose to experience an abundance of freedom in my baldness.*

~ *I choose to attract beauty into my life today.*

~ *I choose to see myself as God sees me, from my soul out with all of its beauty, courage, strength, fortitude, and love.*

~ *I choose to remember my God-given natural state of being. I am created in the image and likeness of God, in health, beauty, and strength.*

Outcome: After losing all of my hair after the first two rounds of chemo (and not doing any EFT), it started to grow back after the fourth round. After the 16th round, I walked into my first radiation treatment and my doctor asked if I was wearing a wig, to which I joyfully replied, "No. It's all mine!"

She said that, in all of her practice, she has never witnessed hair growth with the kind of chemo that I received. Again, I reinforced the power of my focused faith and intention for healing on my physical body, and aligned my energy system with my faith and belief in my God-given ability to heal and restore.

2. *EFT setup statement: Before taking any medication inside my body throughout the five years of treatment, I said, "Even though these 'white coats' have told me that I can have up to 50 different side effects from this medication (or treatment), I choose to love all of me and accept positive energy and benefits from this substance!"*

I would specifically name the medication or treatment I was taking for a full EFT tapping round. Then, I would follow it up with another EFT tapping round using the positive choices I wanted to make and being very specific with some of the side effects:

~ *I choose to surprise myself with an overabundance of mental calm and focus.*

~ *I choose to embrace the positive benefits of chemotherapy and give my body permission to let go of everything that does not benefit my health and restoration.*

~ *Even though I have been told that this medication can cause mouth sores, nausea, nerve damage, foggy thinking, and hair loss, I give my body permission to maintain its God-given natural state of being: health and restoration. I choose to take back my ability to heal down to the cellular level. I have witnessed my body heal before, and I am willing to have confidence that it can do it again. Because God is with me, all things are possible, including the ability to maintain my health and the strength of my body in spite of this medication.*

Outcome: I have had 12 surgeries, 16 chemotherapy treatments, six weeks of daily radiation, one year of Herceptin, Tomoxifin, and the most powerful antibiotics I could take for a MRSA staph infection. I had hair loss initially, some scarring, and darker skin tone, which looks excellent in light of the third-degree burns on my chest due to the radiation/Herceptin combination.

Now, I am completely symptom-free and have been that way throughout all of my treatments. As I became aware of a symptom, I would surrender my health and intention for complete healing and restoration to God. I would also use the

EFT technique to get my energy frequency aligned with my prayer for healing. I can honestly say that I feel stronger and healthier today than ever before. My energy level continues to amaze me daily.

3. *EFT setup statement: After the mastectomy, I had lost all feeling in my chest and down the inside of my left arm. I said, "Even though I have lost all sensation on my chest because of the double mastectomy, I deeply and completely accept all of me and all of my feelings around this, and I choose to restore and reconnect all of my nerves in my chest area. I give my body permission to do what it needs to do to restore my sense of feeling throughout my entire chest area. Jesus said that, through faith, I am capable of doing the miracles of healing He did on earth and even more in John 14:12."*

Reminder phrases I used as I tapped on the EFT Sequence of Tapping Points:

~ *Nerve damage.*

~ *Disrupted nerves.*

~ *Confused chest wall nerves.*

~ *Traumatized chest nerves.*

~ *Nerve disconnect.*

~ *Stressed numb nerves.*

I would follow up with a "positive choices" tapping round and often another round of tapping on the EFT Sequence of Tapping Points, alternating between my nerve damage followed by my positive choice using the following statements:

~ *Even though my nerves were damaged in the surgery, I choose to surrender all that I am to God's healing presence, and unleash complete nerve restoration throughout my entire chest wall.*

~ *Even though I can't feel my chest, I give my body permission to reconnect and restore every nerve in my chest area. I choose complete restoration of my myelin sheaths (a fatty covering that protects nerve fibers) and all parts of the nerves in my chest area. I trust that God has filled my body with divine healing wisdom. I give my body permission to heal.*

Outcome: I have 80 percent of all feeling in my chest area, and I am going for 100 percent!

4. *EFT setup statements: After the mastectomy, I would often wake up in the middle of the night and reach for my breasts because I still felt that they were on my body. After my mom shared the fact that many cultures do not believe in mirrors because they rob the soul of its true identity, I covered all of my mirrors for a full week to give myself the space to align my soul with God. When I was ready to see myself in the mirror, I used the following statements to help connect my energy system with the source of my true inner beauty and femininity—God shining through my body:*

~ *Even though I am breastless, I deeply and completely love and accept myself anyway. I choose to see myself as God sees me: beautiful and complete, lacking nothing. I am willing to remember that my soul remains untouched by any physical alterations in my earth suit. As my son said, "Don't cry, Mom. Your soul still has hair!"*

~ *Even though I have scars all over my chest, I choose to see them as physical examples of my spiritual truth: I am a victorious, beautiful, courageous, and strong woman who shines brighter than ever. God's greatest gift to me is the reminder of what I am not, which has revealed who I am.*

~ *Even though I stand before this mirror bald and breastless, I give myself permission to feel every emotion around this experience with abundant love, respect, and acceptance of all of me. I choose to look into my eyes and define myself by the radiant beauty that flows from my heart even more abundantly now than ever before in my life.*

Reminder phrases I used as I tapped on the EFT Sequence of Tapping Points:

~ *Bald and breastless.*

~ *The mirror's definition of me.*

~ *Bald.*

~ *Breastless.*

~ *Androgynous.*

~ *Stripped of my femininity.*

~ *Yoda, ET.*

I would follow up with a "positive choices" tapping round:

~ *I choose to feel beautiful.*

~ *I choose to feel courageous.*

~ *I choose to forgive myself and anyone else who has contributed to my baldness and breastlessness.*

~ *I choose to celebrate and honor my soul's beauty.*

~ *I choose to have an abundance of creativity as I come up with different ways to see myself as beautiful.*

~ *I choose to respect and honor my body.*

~ *I choose to vibrate with the frequency of gratitude and love, and I choose to send this to every cell of my beautiful body.*

~ *I choose complete restoration and abundant health all the way down to my DNA!*

This is a very brief overview of EFT. You can find more information and a demonstration on my Website, *www.laurenemiller.com,* and YouTube channel, *www. youtube.com/user/2loveandbeloved/ featured.* You can also learn this technique through my online university at *www.StressSolutionsUniversity.com.*

Grab-and-Go Stress Relief Tips

~ *Be specific. Rather than focusing on a global statement, such as "I am afraid of public speaking," get specific about what fuels the fear and, if possible, when that fear started. For example, "When I was in sixth grade and my classmates laughed at me after I stumbled on the words of the presentation. I am still willing to love and accept myself. I choose to speak easily with confidence, remembering that was then and this is now. I have many more resources available to me today. I choose to surprise myself at how easily I am able to speak in public settings."*

~ *Be consistent. When you identify an issue that has a high emotional charge—one that causes that zzzzzt disconnect feeling in your body—continue to apply the EFT on the issue until you can think about the situation and experience "0" physiological response to it.*

13

Quick Stress Relief Tips That You Can Do in Less Than Five Minutes!

Guard your heart for it is the wellspring of life.
                                                    —*Proverbs 4:23*

There is no feeling, except the extremes of fear and grief, that does not find relief in music.
—George Eliot [Mary Ann Evans], British writer

For this constricted breathing technique exercise, use the EFT tapping procedure described in Chapter 12. When you are stressed out, you experience shallow breathing, which results in less oxygen to your brain and the inability to reason and come up with creative solutions to the situations at hand. You will often say, "I just can't think clearly" or "I feel like I'm in a fog."

Here is a five-step technique to help release constricted breathing in the midst of anxiety:

1. *Breathe out all the way and then relax. You will naturally breathe in.*

2. *Rate your intake. For example, on a scale from 0 to 100 percent, how much of your lung capacity are you using? 50 percent? 75 percent? Take a guess. Usually your guesses are linked to your inner knowledge, which lies in the subconscious awareness. Once you have your percentage, begin tapping on it.*

3. *Say your setup statement while tapping on the karate-chop point or rubbing the sore spots: "Even though I am only breathing at about 50 percent from my perspective, I am willing to love and accept myself and I choose to breathe deeply and easily." Repeat this statement three times.*

4. *Tap on the sequence of points laid out for you in Chapter 12, starting with the eyebrow point, while saying this reminder phrase: "This constricted breathing."*

5. *Check in. Breathe all the way out and then in. Are you still at 50 percent? If you are not at 100 percent, keep tapping the sequence points as you say this new reminder phrase: "This remaining constricted breathing." Repeat this exercise, which usually takes less than five minutes, until you feel that you are using the full capacity of your lungs.*

Spontaneous movement moments

In addition to decreasing inflammation and strengthening the immune system, it is very beneficial to oxygenate the cells. The Mayo Clinic[1] often speaks of the positive benefits of regular movement in life.[2] As proof, a woman recently told me that she lost 15 pounds by simply standing up from her desk and doing a vigorous exercise for one to three minutes at the top of each hour during her workday.

Sharp mind

A Mayo Clinic study suggests that regular exercise (and simple forms of physical activity) actually helps protect the mind against mild cognitive impairment. People with mild cognitive impairment can handle simple, everyday events. However, they have difficulty with the kind of brain activities that require them to recall specific details of a conversation or keep track of upcoming appointments.[3]

Daily walk

According to the medical journal *Neurology*, daily walking was enough to lower significantly the risk of developing vascular dementia—the second most common form of dementia after Alzheimer's disease.[4]

Create your own anchor.

You have the ability to anchor any positive experience to your biology by simply activating as many sensory channels as possible. You can use your imagination or real-life experiences to do this.

For example, while I was visiting my parents in Pennsylvania this past summer, I was standing in my mom's beautiful, expansive flower garden, surrounded by the warmth of the sun. The colors in this garden were breathtakingly vibrant, and a beautiful, sweet-smelling aroma floated through it. Butterflies of every imaginable color, hummingbirds, and chipmunks filled the garden. I was overwhelmed with expansive inner peace, gratitude for my life in that moment, and joy to the point that I had shrills (chills from God's spirit within me) running all over my skin. At the peak state of this spectacularly inspiring sensory experience, I placed my right hand over my heart and took a deep breath.

I am now back in Colorado, working on my computer; however, I now have the ability to resurrect that powerful sensory experience from this past summer in my mom's garden by simply placing my right hand over my heart and taking a deep breath as I close my eyes. For a moment, I can take myself back to that beautiful moment and experience.

This week, create your own positive anchor. Choose a moment when you feel a positive emotional state that you would like to anchor into your body. This can also work with your imagination, as long as you elicit as many sensory modalities as possible.

For example, you may close your eyes and think of a time that you felt profound peace and calm—perhaps you were standing on the beach or in the mountains. Engage your imagination and resurrect your sensory experiences around this memory: What did it look like, feel like, and sound like? Increase your connection to the positive emotional and sensory experiences around this memory and, at the peak state, choose your physical anchor: Make the "OK" sign (touch your thumb to your pointer finger and stick the remaining three fingers upward), clasp your hands together, and place your hand over your heart. Be creative! You will be able to resurrect this positive memory, and the emotions and senses that went with it, any time in your future.

I have used this technique after very exhilarating presentations that I have given when I want to remember the feeling of confidence I experienced around it. Before my next public speaking engagement, I will fire off the anchor of confidence I created for myself by making the OK sign and taking in a deep, relaxing breath as I surrender all to God—and go for it.

Finger release

Squeeze each finger with your opposite hand from the base of each finger out. Imagine pulling out your body's tension through each fingertip as you say a phrase of release, such as "Releasing all tension in my body easily and effortlessly."

After pulling out the tension through each finger on both hands, go back and squeeze each fingertip, and pull until your grip releases as you say, "Releasing remaining tension, releasing remaining tension." Shake both hands when you are done.

Hand grip stress release

Use the technique of gently gripping and releasing using your hands as you work up your legs and then each arm. Link your physical movements with a verbal intention for stress release as you say, "Releasing all tension, self-doubt, worry, and fear, returning to the awareness that God is with me. I am safe, confident, and capable of handling any situation that unfolds before me."

After gripping and releasing down each arm, gently pat up your torso with one hand in the front and go up as far as you can with your other hand on your back. As you pat up your torso, say, "Thank you, God, for my soul, body, and mind." End tapping on the top of your head.

As you breathe out all the way, imagine releasing all fear, doubt, and worry that you may be holding in your body. As you breathe in deeply, imagine filling up your body with the Holy Spirit of God.

Repeat this spiritual breathing three times, out with the negative, in with God, as you say, "God is with me. I am enough just as I am, and all things are possible for me today. What God has done for others is now done easily within my life and more."

End with gripping the soft part of your hand, located between the pointer finger and your thumb, and squeeze as hard as you can in this area. It is oftentimes sore, which can indicate stress in the body. Continue to squeeze this soft part of your hand until the soreness dissipates, breathing deeply. Make sure to switch hands.

Hourly movement

Nothing thrives when stagnant, so get up and move throughout your day. Take a one- to five-minute movement moment every hour. Consider different ways to move when you are in transition and be spontaneous. *Have fun!*

Thoughts are thoughts until you label them.

Life unfolds. You have a thought that arises about what is unfolding before you. You will stay in a place of peace through observation until you label that thought as threatening. As soon as you judge that thought, you give birth to the negative emotion. This all happens so fast that sometimes the only thing that remains is the end negative emotion.

Slow down the process: life...thought...negative label...negative emotion (usually fear, worry, self-doubt, and judgment of self or others). Try slowing down and making the conscious choice for positivity: life...thought...positive label...positive emotion. You form your choices and your life by your thoughts.

Choose wisely, wake up, and be the gatekeeper of your thoughts.

NLP eliciting states of behavior

Perhaps you have heard the phrase "Be the change you want to see." There is a lot of truth to that statement. This week, try it out in your own life. In NLP terms, "elicit the state of behavior you wish to encounter."

The next time you find yourself in a situation where you are stressing out because you feel that you are the only one motivated and willing to take action on the next project or desired goal and you want to motivate the people you are with, try this technique:

1. *Get yourself into the state you wish to experience from the person or people who surround you. For example, if you wish to motivate them, then engage yourself in the emotion of motivation. Think back to a time when you experienced motivation: What did it look and feel like? What did your intonation sound like when you were motivated? Get into the state of behavior you want to elicit.*

2. *Describe a situation when you were motivated to the person or people you want to motivate. Get your emotions behind it as you increase your excitement over the experience of being motivated: "When I feel motivated, I feel like I am on top of the world. I can imagine myself going for what I want with a good, strong feeling of confidence and focus. I can taste success when I connect to the emotional experience of motivation. It's exhilarating!"*

3. *Love elicits love, motivation elicits motivation, positivity elicits positivity, and on and on. Choose your state wisely.*[5]

Guarding your heart

The Institute for HeartMath (*heartmath.org*) in California has concluded that the heart is the most powerful generator of electromagnetic energy in the human body—about 60 times greater than the electrical activity of the brain and 5,000 times greater in strength than the field of the brain. Your cardiac field goes out 8 to 10 feet and beyond from where you stand. Your heart signal is so powerful that it can actually affect the brainwaves of another person.

With this in mind, of course it is the wellspring of life. This is the reason that, when other human beings enter your electromagnetic field, you feel their mood before they open their mouth to speak. When human beings come staggering into your field with the ball and chain of victimization or a sense of entitlement dripping off their energy field, and then they unload verbally onto you, of course you feel drained after they slither away.

Use the following zip-up NLP technique before you step into the unknown social drama at work or at home: Start with both of your hands down at your sides, then raise them up in front of your body as if you are zipping up your energy field and guarding your heart. Do this several times.

As you find yourself encountering a low-energy person, and he or she starts to verbally dump garbage on your site, simply turn your shoulder to guard your heart so you are turned slightly to the side rather than heart to heart. You will notice that you are not as drained at the end of the day when you practice guarding your heart.

New behavior generator

This NLP technique is great to use when you want to jump start your attitude in life or, if you feel inadequate in terms of your skills and abilities, you want to increase your confidence:

1. *Close your eyes and imagine someone whom you want to emulate and who has skills and abilities you would like to experience in your own life.*

2. *Imagine a movie screen in front of you with this person performing all of the things that you would like to accomplish. Imagine that he or she can do the things you want to be able to do naturally and easily.*

3. *Play this movie again as you tune into all of the details of his or her behavior and how comfortable this person is doing what you desire to do easily.*

4. *Observe the colors, sounds, vibrations, intonations, and movements of this person. Notice how this person's freedom of expression and confidence gives him or her a special spark.*

5. *Watch the movie again. This time, imagine putting yourself in this person's role. Repeat the actions, movements, and intonations that you witnessed with your unique essence and personality. Observe yourself stepping into more confidence and self-expression.*

6. *Replay the movie with you in it, and observe how comfortable you are stepping into the attributes that you admired about this person. Allow the feeling of freedom and confidence to absorb into your body.*

7. *Until now, you observed this using your imagination; now, walk inside the movie. Feel, hear, and see everything as you experience each scene from inside this movie. Make it your own and increase the feelings of confidence you desire to resurrect within you.*

8. *As you open your eyes and reenter your life, watch how easily these talents and abilities emerge.*[6]

Bag kick

Your anger needs to have a healthy method of release. My background is martial arts, so I will often hit and kick the bag in my basement. (This was a perfect solution for me when I was diagnosed with cancer.)

Silent scream

Go into the bathroom and, without making any noise (so you can do this anywhere), pretend to scream, tense your body, clench your fists, and let it rip. Stomp your feet quickly. My EFT practitioner gave me this tool when I was going through cancer and divorce. I would usually end up laughing at myself, which has tons of healing benefits—not to mention diffusing the anger!

Noodle release

Buy yourself a swimming pool noodle (a Styrofoam flotation device, usually found at Target or K-Mart) and cut it in half. The next time you are ticked off about something or with someone, take your noodle and whack your bed, couch, or any object that will not be damaged. You can verbalize your anger as you let it out. Again, I usually end up cracking myself up doing this, which instantly puts life in to perspective. This is an awesome stress relief technique for children. When my daughter gets mad, she will often say, "Mom, I just need to go get the noodle!"

Morning jump-start

Commit five to 15 minutes each morning to movement. Each morning I do situps, pushups, and squats to get the blood flowing.

Create your own 15-minute warm up before you start your day and stick to it! Often, we don't stick to a workout plan because we have placed requirements around the workout experience: "In order for this to count, I have to go to the gym and work out for one hour. I don't have an hour, so forget it."

Drop all expectations and time constraints around the experience, and just get out and move. Get rid of your scale! Remember: "Whatever you focus on *grows bigger!*" Love and accept yourself right where you are, and *then* move toward what you want in life.

Balls-of-your-feet bounce

This is a great spontaneous movement moment, which can be done at the top of each hour during your day. Rub on the sore spots mentioned in Chapter 12. Start at the two spots located to the right and left of the U-shaped dip in your clavicle at the base of your throat. Go 3 inches down and over on each side, and you will find the sore spots.

As you bounce up and down on the balls of your feet while rubbing these spots, you help lymphatic drainage and get a quick boost of energy.

Jumping in place

In tae kwon do, they use a movement in the "sparring stance" where you lightly jump up and down for one to five minutes. This will spark your energy and get the blood flow going as well as increase oxygen to the brain, which results in clarity of thinking and focus. You also release fluid buildup around your organs.

Spontaneous musical dance

Music and dance flow from the soul and connect the hearts of humanity. Spontaneous movement throughout your day sparks creativity and reconnects you to your sense of humor. Bring more music into your life. Start today and create an environment within your being in which inspiration and creativity flourish.

Come up with your own special victory dance in life. The psychological and physiological benefits that come with dancing and singing—powerful forms of instant stress relief—are endless.

If you don't feel like dancing because you're angry about something, do the "noodle release" technique (described on page 142) and start dancing. Have fun with it and explore your space. When you really let yourself go and dance during your day, laughter often follows, which adds to the stress relief benefits.

Knee lifts and stretching

At the top of the hour each day for one to 10 minutes, stand up and begin to stretch any way that feels good to your body. Remaining flexible in life leads to the ability to adjust easily to new situations and challenges. Keep your body aligned with the positive energy that flows from flexibility.

As you stretch, breathe out completely and then relax. You will naturally breathe in deeply. Add knee lifts while holding your stomach in to increase the blood flow and deep breathing.

Thymus tap

This technique is very powerful when you fear the future. Thymus tapping helps to realign your energy system with inner confidence.

Use your fingertips to tap lightly on your thymus, located approximately 2 inches down from the lowest point in the U-shaped dip at the base of your throat. Lightly tap as you say:

I have faith and confidence in God. My future is secure. I am secure.

Continue to repeat this for one to three minutes. If you do not feel aligned with this statement, try:

I am willing to have faith and confidence in God. I am willing to explore the possibility that my future is secure. I am willing to believe that I am secure.

HeartMath

The Institute of HeartMath has good information and quick stress relief techniques, which were very powerful throughout my treatment.[7]

"The core of the HeartMath philosophy is that the heart, physically and metaphorically, is the key to tapping into an intelligence that can provide us with fulfillment. Science has shown that the heart communicates with the body and brain on various levels.

"Some of the earliest recorded civilizations speak of the heart as embodying intelligence. Modern science has tended to consider this point of view metaphorical. Doc Childre, founder of the Institute of HeartMath in Boulder Creek, California, has produced scientific evidence to back up the 'intelligent heart' theory." [8]

Many major corporations, such as Motorola and Hewlett-Packard, and the U.S. military, use HeartMath to help their employees return to mental and emotional inner balance.

The Freeze-Frame, which is the simplest of the HeartMath tools, allows a major shift in perception. It gives you the ability to shift out of the jungle that is created by your thoughts back into your heart.

When you connect with a moment in your life that resonates with positive feelings, and then re-enter the situation that was causing you stress, you will often find that your perception of the situation shifts to the positive.

Remember: You always have control over your perception of the event and your response to it. Perhaps by giving yourself this one-minute shift, you will activate insights needed to come up with a creative solution or the strength to release the stress and move on; perhaps you will feel calm and focused.

Become aware of any changes within, remembering that whatever you focus on *grows bigger*. The one-minute Freeze-Frame from HeartMath gives you the opportunity to step back from the stressor and reconnect within to the beauty in life.

You can find the Freeze-Frame technique in *Transforming Anger*.

Quick Coherence Technique

You can do the Quick Coherence Technique by HeartMath anytime, anywhere, and in less than one minute. Use this technique when you feel stress, negative thoughts, perceptions, or emotions creeping up in your body. When you start to feel overwhelmed and drained by your to-do list, or pressured by your deadlines, stop and bring yourself back to inner peace by following this powerful three-step technique:

1. **Heart Focus.** *Focus your attention on the area around your heart and the area in the center of your chest. If you prefer, the first couple of times you try it, place your hand over the center of your chest to help keep your attention in the heart area.*

2. **Heart Breathing.** *Breathe deeply, but normally, and imagine that your breath is coming in and going out through your heart area. Continue breathing with ease until you find a natural inner rhythm that feels good to you.*

3. **Heart Feeling.** *As you maintain your heart focus and heart breathing, activate a positive feeling. Recall a positive feeling, a time when you felt good inside, and try to re-experience the feeling. One of the easiest ways to generate a positive, heart-based feeling is to remember a special place you've been to or the love you feel for a close friend or family member or treasured pet. This is the most important step."* [9]

Moving and shaking therapy

This healing technique is used worldwide to release inner toxins, emotionally and physically. All of the animal kingdom shakes. You have heard the phrase "just shake it off," referring to letting something go that is holding you back in life. Yet, you are now rigid as you have grown into your adult experience.

What happened? Perhaps you received a message that said, "Stop squirming around like that. Sit still!" You made the connection that random, sporadic movement is not safe.

Consider life as flow and movement that exist in nature. Creation responds to the elements around it, like the wind and the water. Flexibility and flow allow for expansion and growth.

Before you enter this world, you are moving within the womb. As you move through your first years of life, you are constantly exploring different ways of movement and expression until someone tells you to stop moving. As you get older, you become more and more rigid until you lie down, leave your rigid body behind, and return to the flexibility of your spirit.

Do you want health and vitality to return? Start reconnecting with movement on a daily basis. How many new ways can you move through your day? I tried skipping down the grocery store aisle the other day and ended up getting the benefits of the laughter that went with it! Return to the playfulness that accompanies exploring different ways to move in this world.

Shaking—a release and a dance between the rest and arousal states—has profound healing benefits. You can shake your body at any time. You see athletes doing this before games to loosen everything up.

The next time you experience a negative memory, an emotion, or a perception, including your inner critic, try this technique:

> ~ *Close your eyes and imagine all of that emotion being concentrated in one part of your body.*

~ *Start to shake that part of your body and imagine being able to move that emotion or memory down through your legs and arms, and right out of your hands and feet.*

~ *Do this several times until you feel the inner calm return.*

~ *You can shake while lying down.*

~ *After shaking it off, return to the rest cycle. Lie down on the ground, preferably outside on the grass.*

~ *Do an internal scan and look for any remaining fear, doubt, or worry. Imagine the residue from any negative emotion flowing out of your body into the energy of the Earth.*

God created the Earth, and it resonates with the power of His healing touch and abundant life. Allow your fears, doubts, and worries to be consumed by the energy of life that surrounds you.

After going through extensive treatment for cancer and a divorce in less than two years, I had a lot of "shaking off" to do. I am learning more about shaking therapy and how the Bushmen of Africa have used this technique as medicine to heal emotionally and physically on all levels.

The next time you feel inner anxiety, practice shaking it off!

Thymus thump

A doctor friend of mine from Costa Rica shared the following technique, which is practiced in Peru while watching the sunrise:

~ *Take your fist and lightly tap on your thymus, located 2 to 3 inches down from the U-shaped dip at the base of your neck.*

~ *As you tap on your chest, exhale rhythmically, "HA HA HA, HA HA HA, HA HA HA, HA HA HA," until you have pushed all of the air out of your lungs.*

~ *Continue to thump lightly on your chest as you inhale deeply.*

~ *Repeat this technique for three to five minutes.*

You will find that you experience clarity of thinking and renewed energy. This technique can be done throughout the day.

Stressor/action sheet

A lot of your daily stress revolves around your fear that you won't get it all done. You will find that, by writing out the stressor and action on paper (even if the action is to release or accept what is, or decide that you will take action tomorrow), you will feel empowered versus powerless when challenging events pop up.

~ *Make a stressor/action sheet and carry it with you. Take a piece of paper and fold it in half. At the top of the left column, write "Stressor"; at the top of the right column, write "Action."*

~ *As an event or situation comes up in your day and causes you any internal anxiety, write it down under "Stressor."*

~ *Ask yourself, "What can I do about this right now?" and write it down under "Action."*

Your sense of humor

Rediscover and nurture your sense of humor. Commit yourself to at least five to 10 minutes of laughter each day, even if it's fake. Seriously ill people have been healed because of their choice to laugh every day.

When I was diagnosed with cancer, I remember making the choice to laugh more every day simply because I felt better inside. I remember watching as many funny movies as I could get my hands on.

If you can laugh at life and yourself, you create an environment within and around you where the lightness of life replaces seriousness. You may have the belief that productivity and success flow from seriousness. Productivity actually flows from *not* taking yourself or life too seriously. This maintains a lighthearted outlook where creativity, inspiration, and purpose flourish.

Laughter has physiological and psychological benefits. Laughter reduces stress hormones, strengthens the immune system, and lowers blood pressure. Laughter instantly stimulates a positive outlook on life. The medical world is looking at laughter as a possible cure for asthma, depression, and even cancer. People who laugh a lot are less likely to experience stress in their life. Nurture your sense of humor. You can't be stressed out and laughing at the same time!

Laughter is a physical release as well as an excellent tool to shift your perception away from the stress. Having a lighthearted perspective offers you an incredible opportunity to enter that little gap of empowerment where you can shift your perception of a stressful event in life from a place of fear, doubt, and worry to an opportunity for learning and growth.

Similar to the act of smiling, studies show that you still get all of the positive benefits from laughter—even if it's fake. Act your way into feeling. Fake laughter and, before you know it, you'll be cracking up for real! I tried this technique the other night and found myself crying because I was laughing so hard over my attempt at the "fake laugh."[10]

Conscious breathing

When a human being is stressed out, oftentimes one of the first physiological responses is shallow breathing. Awareness is a key ingredient when making a conscious shift back to inner calm.

Here is one of my quick techniques. I learned it while going through the experience of radiation. I felt that the chemo would help my tumors to shrink. In spite of my resistance to do six weeks of radiation, I found myself lying under the radiation machine while everyone ran out of the room.

That was an obvious red flag to me, and the realization that I had made the wrong decision to do this treatment haunted me through the 30 rounds of radiation. Because I was still on chemo in the midst of the radiation treatment, I didn't know that I would end up with third-degree burns all over my chest. I had open wounds for more than a year and several moments of anxiety in the midst of it all. After 14 surgeries, my surgeon successfully grafted my back onto my front. Most days, I don't know if I'm coming or going!

I say this from a place of observation rather than victimization. I believe that *all* things can work for an ultimate good in life simply by our choice of response to them. As I was alone with that radiation machine, I remember saying, "Even though I am told I could have negative side effects from this treatment, I made the decision to get the radiation anyway. I give my body permission to respond to the positive benefits, and to release everything that does not promote healing and restoration in my body. I am created to heal and I give my body permission to easily return to my natural state of health and strength."

I used the following technique to help relax my body, and I still use it today:

~ *Slowly breathe out all the way.*

~ *Take one finger and press it on the side of one nostril, and slowly and deeply breathe in.*

~ *Using the same finger, switch it to the other nostril and press it down, blocking the air flow out of that nostril, as you breathe out completely.*

~ *Continue gently closing that same nostril as you breathe in deeply.*

~ *Switch again and close the other nostril, gently pressing on the side of your nose and breathing out all of the way through the open nostril.*

~ *Continue gently closing that same nostril as you breathe in deeply.*

~ *Switch again and close the other nostril, gently pressing on the side of your nose and breathing out all the way through the open nostril.*

~ *Continue this cycle until you notice a sense of calm and focus return.*

Remember that God used the spoken word to bring forth creation. You have the ability to do the same. Choose a phrase or two that speak to your desired state of being. Proclaim these statements before and after the conscious breathing technique.

As you breathe in and out, imagine releasing the tension and breathing in clarity of focus as you pull from your timeline moments (situations, experiences, or events from your lifetime) when you have overcome, moved through, and grown in the midst of perceived trials.

The following are a few statements I have used during moments I have entertained fear, doubt, and worry:

~ *I choose to release all fear, doubt, and worry. Even though I have identified with the struggle in my life, I give my body my permission to return easily to its natural state of peace and healing.*

~ *I am willing to remember my God-given ability to overcome any perceived challenge in my life.*

~ *I was created to create. I give the Spirit of the Living God permission to create healing and restoration within my body, along with the confidence and courage to remember that I am safe, complete, and enough, just as I am.*

~ *I have been overwhelmed before and have experienced the return to peace and confidence in the midst of it. I choose to return to peace and confidence again now.*

~ *I am willing to focus on my desired result.*

Remember this truth: Things have to be the way they are until they don't. Go within and work your way out. You have done this many times in your life and you can do it again.

Much of your anxiety flows from your hard drive, which says, "In order to be happy in life, I need to be perfect." Practice happiness, which flows from the inner knowing that you have already made it in this life, and there is no need to prove that to any human being, including yourself. Drop back into the remembrance that you are enough, just as you are, and surrounded by God. Just as a fish in water, no matter where your mind swims, even to the depth of despair, you are surrounded by the ocean of God's love for you.

Take action

"Practice" is a word that has built-in grace. As you go through the suggested stress relief techniques, consider this as an opportunity to practice identifying and adjusting your perception of threatening situations in your life.

Choose to be a curious observer or the watcher of your life as events and people's responses unfold before you. Notice when your body feels tense or anxious. How do you hold tension in your body? Once you identify where you hold tension, ask yourself what emotion is behind that physical expression of tension. Three main emotions—*fear, self-doubt,* and *worry*—fuel stress.

The next time you become aware of something in your life experience that you have processed through your five senses, and conclude that it threatens your sense of safety and well-being, dismantle it by asking yourself these questions:

~ *"Where am I expressing this perceived threat in my body?"*

~ *"When did I first become aware of tension in my body and restricted thinking (that is, obsessively repeating a negative thought)?"*

~ *"Are my shoulders tight?"*

~ *"Do I have tension in my jaw?"*

~ *"Is my throat tightening up?"*

Is it fear? If so, of what are you afraid? Is it a future event happening or not happening? If you were to guess what initial thought set this fear in motion, what would it be? Not being acknowledged? Not being seen? Not receiving approval? Is it coming from a desire for a certain position or status, or different life experience?

Remember that nothing increases stress within the body faster than being in life and your mind is in the future or past, lamenting over your need to know why things happen as they do or how things are going to turn out for you in the future.

What would you need to remember in order for that fear to vanish? What would you need to know in order for you to feel secure being present to the life in front of your face? Step into imagining your life without that fear or need to know. What would you imagine, feel, or hear in your life differently if you did not have that fear? How much space in your thinking would you gain to create new openings, options, and solutions if you released that fear from your radar? What would it take to release that fear and return to inner peace and confidence?

Write down your insights and answers to the following question: "In order to feel safe and confident in this situation, I would need to know or remember."

Imagine that situation. As a result of remembering and focusing on what you just wrote down—what you would need to know or remember in order to feel confident in a certain situation—now imagine stepping into the positive attributes you have recovered, and write down what you feel, see, and hear differently by knowing this.

Explore the confidence you would know and feel as you picture yourself stepping into the situation in which you would like to feel more confident. Increase your awareness of what it feels like to be confident. What do you look and sound like when you are confident? How do people respond to you when you are confident?

Anchor this confident feeling at the peak state, utilizing your imagination around *you* being confident. Take your right fist, tap a few times on the left side of your chest, and say aloud, "Confidence." You have now created a physical anchor—a powerful

NLP technique that you can use in any situation to evoke the imaginative state of confidence you just created.

If you experience self-doubt in your life, dismantle the experience. The more specific you can get, down to the basic fuel behind the self-doubt, the quicker you will be able to adjust your perception of you as you face different threatening situations.

What part of *you* do you doubt? Is it your ability to excel? Handle the situation? Survive? Heal? Get people to agree with your point of view? Provide for your family? Create a healthy relationship? Perform? Gain approval? Be all things to all people? Make a certain amount of money? Forgive another person? Forgive yourself? Finish your to-do list by the end of the week? Meet a deadline? Finish a project? Relax? Let go? Release?

I have often heard this statement from clients: "I can't let go of this," to which I reply, "Let go of what? What specifically can't you let go of?"

After more clarity of focus is established, we then explore re-establishing the client's awareness and alignment with who they are—not what they do or how people respond to them in their life.

Specifically identify your self-doubt, and then explore the following questions:

~ *"What would it take to release doubting my ability to handle this situation?"*

~ *"What do I need to remember from my time line that would help me regain a sense of confidence in this specific situation?"*

~ *"When was the first time I can remember having this doubt about myself? How old was I? Where was I?"*

~ *"What specifically did I feel, see, and hear during that first moment of doubting myself?"*

~ *Based on the skills and insights I have gained in my life since that first moment of self-doubt, if I could go back and dialogue with myself when I first experienced this self-doubt, what would I want to say to myself?"*

~ *"What would I have wanted to know back then that I know now, which would have boosted my confidence in who I am?"*

~ *"If I remembered this insight or wisdom, how would that have shifted my choices and reactions to life?"*

~ *"Imagining that I have full confidence in my ability to excel and handle any situation in life, what would I notice to be different in my relationship with God? With other people? At work? With my inner self-talk?"*

Practice waking up tomorrow and act your way into feeling confident. What would you need to remember about yourself in order to feel confident and capable? Pull experience from your life when you had a moment of self-confidence and courage.

Ask yourself, "If I feel completely confident in myself and in the gifts and skills with which God has blessed me, how will that specifically play out in my day today?" Write down what you will notice, see, experience, and feel.

Do you experience worry in your life? Do you feel strangled? Stifled? Restricted in any way? About what specific thing are you worried? Tomorrow? Today? Yesterday? Clothes? House? Job? Are you worried for yourself? Your children? Your coworker? That you will not have enough? Be enough? That you won't accept yourself if you don't get something accomplished? That people won't accept you if you don't accomplish specific tasks? Worried you can't do something? Lose weight? Recover from an illness? An addiction? Move past a phobia? Worried that someone is out to get you? That you won't reach or accomplish a desired goal? Let people down? Let yourself down? Not measure up to the standards you have on your internal list, which says, "I will love myself when..." or "I will accept myself when..." or "Nothing ever seems to work out for me and I am worried that nothing ever will"? In relationships? Spiritually? Your career? Physically?

Specifically identify and write down your worry, such as "I am worried about (insert worry) specifically because..."

Once you have identified what is creating the worry in that specific incidence, ask yourself the following questions:

~ *"What would need to shift in my thinking in order to release my worry around this specific information?"*

~ *"Is there any information from my past that I am deleting, which contradicts this worry?"*

For example, let's say that, after a breakup, your worry is that you will not be able to find someone in your life with whom to share a healthy, happy relationship. Begin to scan your time line and tune into specific information that contradicts this impoverished view of reality.

As soon as you find the information, a shift will occur in your thinking. You will begin to return to your inner knowing that you are more than capable of connecting positively with people in life, which will then shift your approach to the people you meet.

Your confidence will begin to emerge. You have that RAS in your brain, whose sole purpose is behavioral motivation.

The RAS will tune onto whatever you choose to focus. If it's worrying about not having some situation turn out the way you want, or that you will not get what you think you need in order to feel fulfilled, capable, and loved, then it will tune into pieces of information that back up that worry thinking. You are the programmer of the RAS, so choose wisely for what you want to start seeing more of in your life.

The RAS is the Reticular Activating System located close to the brain stem and responsible for behavioral motivation. It tunes into whatever your focus is, and hunts and gathers information from your environment that supports whatever your perception is at the moment. It can be your greatest friend or your worst enemy, depending on what you choose to focus on in life. For example, whether your focus on what is working out for you or what's not working out, your choice of focus makes all the difference in the outcome. You are the gatekeeper of your RAS so choose your focus wisely.

Another question to ponder is this: What is the upside for holding onto this worry? How does worrying about this situation serve you? Believe it or not, you will stop worrying when you figure out the answer to that question. Once you can identify the fuel behind your choice to worry continually about a specific situation, you are in a powerful position to tune into a different choice of response to that segment of your life. What information would be helpful to remember in order to step out of this troubled state of mind?

You are not a victim in this situation. You have the God-given ability to release the worry response you are giving to the situation at hand. You may resist that concept because you are so deeply entrenched in a worry response to life. Whom would you be if you did not worry? What would your life look like if you made the decision to abandon the worry response? How much space would be created in your life if you let go of worrying? Did you know that the Greek word for worry, *merimnao*, means to "divide the mind," and the German word for worry, *sorge*, means "to strangle"?

The Bible contains a powerful invitation: "Do not be anxious about anything, but in everything, by prayer and petition, with thanksgiving, present your requests to God. And the peace of God, which transcends all understanding, will guard your hearts and your minds in Christ Jesus." (Philippians 4:6–7)

Practice responding to your worries with a conscious prayer of release: "Even though I am worried, I choose God over this fear. You have created the heavens and the earth, and You live within and through me. Therefore, I thank you that *all* things are possible for me. This includes my ability to return to inner peace in the midst of any perceived threat in my life."

Grab-and-Go Stress Relief Tips

~ *Honor your own uniqueness.*

~ *Have fun with the different techniques. Pick one or two each week and see what feels good to you.*

~ *Reconnect with your sense of humor on a daily basis.*

~ *Practice living life from a curious and fascinated perspective.*

14

Self-Appreciation Notebook

As mentioned in the section entitled "Action #2: Release the Inner Critic" (Chapter 8), one of the essential ingredients for a stress-free life experience is letting go of all negativity.

You can do the following five-minute exercise in the evenings. Because what you focus on in your day *grows bigger*, this activity gives you the opportunity to focus on what you love about yourself—not in a prideful sense, but in a very compassionate, humble sense of appreciation for you.

As you start to recognize and appreciate the little things you love about yourself, you will be more apt to recognize the beautiful gifts and talents in the lives of those around you. This inner connection of appreciation creates a positive environment, which is conducive to healthy communication void of all defensive behavior. Defensive behavior is a direct result of low self-esteem, which flows from forgetting your worth and lovability.

Take action

After my hair fell out from the chemo, I remember reading a beautiful children's story to my 10-year-old child entitled *The Velveteen Rabbit*. We got to the part when two of the main characters—a stuffed rabbit and a horse, both toys of a young boy—had a very insightful conversation:

"What is Real?" asked the Rabbit one day, when they were lying side by side near the nursery fender.

"Real isn't how you are made," said the Skin Horse. "It's a thing that happens to you when a child loves you for a long, long time, not just to play with, but really loves you, then you become Real."

"Does it hurt?" asked the Rabbit.

"Sometimes," said the Skin Horse, for he was always truthful. "When you are Real you don't mind being hurt."

"Does it happen all at once, like being wound up," he asked, "or bit by bit?"

"It doesn't happen all at once," said the Skin Horse. "You become. It takes a long time. That's why it doesn't often happen to people who break easily or have sharp edges, or who have to be carefully kept. Generally, by the time you are Real, most of your hair has been loved off, your eyes drop out and you get loose in the joints and very shabby. But these things don't matter at all, because once you are Real you can't be ugly, except to people who don't understand."

Weeks passed, and the little Rabbit grew very old and shabby, but the boy loved him just as much. He loved him so hard that he loved all his whiskers off, and the pink lining to his ears turned gray, and his brown spots faded. He even began to lose his shape, and he scarcely looked like a rabbit any more, except to the boy. To him he was always beautiful, and that was all that the little Rabbit cared about. He didn't mind how he looked to other people, because the nursery magic had made him Real, and when you are Real shabbiness doesn't matter.[1]

At this point in the story, my son smacked his hand down on the page, looked me right in the eye, and put his other hand on top of my bald head.

"Mom! Look at this! You are the Rabbit! We loved you so much that your hair fell out."

I will never forget this moment because it reminded me once again that the richness of my life experience flows directly from my ability to love and be loved as I finish my journey on Earth.

Practice the following NLP technique I learned during my training at the American University of NLP. You can only give out in relationships what you take time to put in, resurrect, and ground within yourself. I invite you to give to others from the overflow of love and confidence you nurture within yourself.

This technique will help you anchor self-appreciation by seeing yourself through the eyes of someone who loves you, just as you are and for whom you are, not because of something you do or don't do in your life. It will help you access the appreciation for yourself that others have for you along with building inner confidence. I use it in my own life when I forget to align myself with love and appreciation for the beautiful creation that God has made me to be on Earth:

~ *Choose someone who loves you unconditionally, or think of someone who sincerely appreciates you resulting from of a kindness you have shown him or her in life.*

~ *Imagine that you are sitting at a desk in a room, writing your autobiography. As you look up, you see the person who loves or appreciates you looking at you through the other side of a glass door.*

~ *Float your awareness outside of the room, and imagine standing next to this special person. Observe yourself writing your autobiography from that perspective. Write down any specific things you notice about yourself.*

~ *Enter the body of the person who appreciates and loves you, and see yourself through his or her eyes of acceptance and unconditional love. Be still and imagine how this person loves you without conditions. Allow yourself to sink into those feelings of love and appreciation for the beautiful person that you are. See yourself as they see you. See yourself as God sees you: beautifully and wonderfully created in love.*

~ *After you have lingered in those positive feelings of love and appreciation, float back into your body, and write down all of the qualities and aspects you heard and saw about yourself that you experienced through the eyes and heart of that special person.*

~ *Reflect on your life. Imagine all of the possible current situations as well as future situations when you will want to access your awareness of the love and appreciation that you experienced through the eyes of the one who loves you, just as you are.*

Finish the following sentence at the end of each day with one to three things you appreciated about yourself:

I love the way I:

Write it down every day and reflect on your findings at the end of each week.

Grab-and-Go Stress Relief Tip

~ *You are created—beautifully and wonderfully—in love, for love, and by love. Love is all you remember at the end of this journey on Earth, so start investing today.*

15

The Power of Gratitude and Random Acts of Kindness

As a practice to help you live life on purpose, at the end of each day, ask yourself six questions:

1. *How was I a blessing to those around me today?*
2. *How did I offer love and kindness to the world around me?*
3. *How was I blessed by others today?*
4. *In what ways did I experience love and kindness today?*
5. *Is there anything in my actions or words that I would have liked to infuse with more love and compassion?*
6. *What are three things I was grateful for today?*

One positive connection a day

At one point or another along your journey, you have heard about the importance of gratitude. One of the quickest ways to motivate and inspire those around you is to practice gratitude and random acts of kindness. This is one of the quickest ways to form a connection among human hearts. A kind word of appreciation, gratitude, a humble heart, and random acts of kindness are the keys that unlock connection instantly between human beings.

Several times throughout my journey with cancer, I would venture out into the world bald. The response of those around me gave me insight into the depth of compassion contained within the human heart.

I experienced many random acts of kindness. On several occasions, the person in front of me in line at the coffee shop bought my tea. I had several meals completely paid for at restaurants and I received tons of cards every day. One time, a policeman actually tore up my ticket and said, "Have a nice day!" when he saw me walking toward my car. I will never forget the abundance of compassion and kindness poured out in my life from people whom I had never met.

Input/output…output/input

How you love and nurture yourself flows out into the world around you *and* whatever you put out into the world comes right back at you. Love evokes love. Fear evokes fear.

In every moment, you choose the fuel to move in this life. Love and fear exist together; when love is your focus, it consumes all fear. It is not an either/or experience. Knowing this will give you more compassion with yourself when you are fueled by fear.

Fear is the result of forgetting how loved, capable, and worthy you are. The God of all creation is with you; therefore, you have the tools and skills to create your response to life. When you remember that love is constant within you and consumes all traces of fear, you return to remembering the power of the Holy Spirit within you. Once again, love will fuel all of your actions and responses in this world.

The next time you feel fear, in any of its deceptive forms, remember that you are simply forgetting your worth, strength, and lovability in that moment. Fear is the absence of remembering yourself as connected to God. Return to remembrance by saying the following statement:

> *Even though I am feeling fearful in this moment and incapable of handling this situation, I am willing to be moved by God's Holy Spirit in spite of my lack of awareness of the power that dwells within my being. I give You permission to move me back to remembering how capable, valuable, and loved I am.*

Have you ever noticed that, when you are moving with a lighthearted spirit that feels secure and loved, the entire world around you seems to join in the fun and you notice all that *is* working out for you? On the other hand, when you enter life with criticism, negative thoughts, and self-judgment, the entire world around you seems to reflect those views right back at you.

You can choose how you want to respond to life. Your choice makes all the difference in the outcome. Connection in life creates an experience of well-being and inner peace. Practice random acts of kindness throughout your day and observe the good feelings you experience because of them. After a random act of kindness, you will instantly forget about the stress in your life. All things beautiful in this life flow from the moments when you connect to love.

Take action

Make at least one positive connection—a random act of kindness—each day and record it. "Today's positive connection made me feel…" Remember that whatever you reflect upon *grows bigger* and you will experience more of it in life.

Grab-and-Go Stress Relief Tips

~ *You cannot be depressed and grateful at the same time. Gratitude walks hand in hand with a kind and compassionate heart. Human beings gravitate toward those who live in the energy of humility and who have mastered the ability to speak their truth with love.*

~ *Whatever you reflect upon at the end of the day travels with you into the next day. When your reflections are fueled by your desire to learn how to grow in the ways of love, you will start to see more of that which you love and appreciate in life. This is truly a transformational life practice.*

Conclusion:
A Moment of Peace

Your perspective in life is extremely innovative and expedient at gathering information to support its view. If your perspective is one of negativity, such as "Nothing ever works out for me," then evidence of that view will start showing up all around you. If your perspective is one of love, gratitude, and appreciation, which says, "Everything unfolds perfectly for me in life," then the evidence will appear to support that view. Remember: You choose every day of your life on Earth.

As you remember your worth and how loved you are by God, just as you are, you will begin to see your world light up around you. You will begin to recall that fear is simply contained in the moments when you forget your value. God delights in you. When you choose to delight in you, you will delight in the experience of interacting with those around you.

Every experience contains the invitation for learning and growth in the ways of love. With each new dawn, your deepest desire is to know yourself as loved, accepted, capable, and worthy. The truth is that you are all of these. When you forget this, you become vulnerable to the experience of lack and scarcity, where the phantoms of fear, doubt, and worry slither around your mind.

During my extensive medical treatments, I had a few opportunities to experience a lifting of my spirit out of my body. When my body was filled with the MRSA staph infection, at one moment I felt the warmth of that experience being in my body, and the next I was standing next to my body.

This was the second time I was graced with an out-of-body experience. During the first time, I experienced heart failure after a difficult chemo treatment. I walked away both times with a clear understanding of what is truly essential on this journey of life.

Two things remain: love and your experience with love. You forgot that every experience that happens within your life is an opportunity to remember your purpose here on Earth. You forgot this awareness as your obsessive need to be told that you are enough, that you are capable, and most deeply that you are loved and accepted, just as you are, took a hold of you.

That's okay. Simply give yourself the space and compassion to remember what you forgot: You are loved, capable, and worthy. When I popped out of my Earth suit during my out-of-body experience, I instantly knew that I was safe. I remember almost chuckling at all of the antics I put myself through, worrying about my well-being. Even as I observed the doctors' frantic attempts to revive me, I felt compassion for their unnecessary fear and doubt around the thought that I was not going to live.

The truth is that I am okay and you are okay—even in death, which is really a phantom fear. It is profound to remember who you are: a spirit, who always knows itself to be loved and capable, connected to God. This is your natural state of being. You simply forget when you farm out your sense of identity to a person, condition, or experience.

God created your body to heal. You witnessed this the first time you scraped your knee and a scab formed, only to reveal new, healthy skin in a matter of days. Your natural state is health and wellness.

The same holds true for love. Low self-esteem, comparison, and judgment of yourself and others flow from amnesia when you forget that your natural state is love. Any time you compare yourself to another human being, it's the same as saying, "You have something I need in order to love and accept myself." As you remember your natural state, you remember what you value most in this life.

When tragedy hits, people remember instantly that the connections made in love on this Earth are all that truly matter. Several family members, who were in the middle of the September 11, 2001, trauma of the attacks on the Twin Towers, said that people left behind all material possessions, including shoes, and ran with their phones, trying to call the people they love.

Our natural state of connection and safety fuels our sense of well-being. All of the meetings at the office, and the encounters with people in and out of your day, contain sacred invitations to expand and grow into what your spirit already knows.

Stop walking past those moments of invitation, and remember who you are and what your purpose is on Earth. You are created to grow beautifully and wonderfully in the ways of love with the gift of each new dawn. Don't wait until you take your last breath to remember that inner peace is a choice and available to you as you remember your worth and lovability.

It comes down to the experience of loving and being loved when reflecting on the moments that truly move you in your life, which are loving God, yourself, or those around you. The business deal does not excite you. Look deeper.

You are always invited to connect to something deeper, such as remembering a piece of you, which is connected to God within and which inspires you to create, move, and take action for a greater good in this world.

I have often worked with clients who have said, "I have been this way my whole life," "Everyone in my family has this condition," or "This pain is so deep. I feel I have such a long way to go before I'm healed."

Remember this truth: Healing of any kind is not dependent upon time or intensity. Jesus revealed this truth many times, as He would ask those who received a healing, "How long have you been this way?" (Mark 9:21) and "What do you want me to do for you?" (Mark 10:51). After the healing took place, in a single moment of belief, and no matter how long the person was living with the disease or condition, he would often say, "Go, your faith has made you well" (Mark 10:52).

You are now equipped with a toolbox, filled with techniques and practices to help you help yourself remember that your natural state is love, health, and inner peace, which gives birth to confidence, creativity, and purpose.

Don't stress out about memorizing all of the tools. This is Grab-and-Go stress relief, so have fun with it! Sift through the techniques and Grab-and-Go tips. Choose a few each week to practice. Maintain a spirit of curiosity and fascination. Keep what works for you and integrate them into your life.

Remember that, with each new dawn of life, you have an opportunity to learn how to love better. In the end, love is all that truly matters.

I will end with sharing my video entitled "A Moment of Peace." I created this video in 2010 in the midst of finding out that I had another tumor in my uterus. They were checking to see if I had ovarian cancer; all tests came back benign. For me, it was just another opportunity to surrender all to God and return to inner peace. To see the video, please visit my YouTube channel at *www.youtube.com/2loveandbeloved*

Grab-and-Go Stress Relief Tips

~ *At the sunset of this life, two reflections will remain:*

1. *How well did I love God, others, and myself?*
2. *How did I influence those who crossed my path for a greater good?*

~ *Hair, breasts, or anything outside of you does not have the power to define you unless you give that power away.*

~ *Your perceptions form your thoughts. Your thoughts form your choices. Your choices form your life. Choose wisely.*

~ *Stress is the natural state when you forget your value, your capability, and how loved you are, just as you are.*

~ *You have already made it in this life. There is no need for recognition or acknowledgment along with the antics you play to get them.*

~ *You are safe and connected, even in death.*

~ *You can handle anything that unfolds before you in this life. You simply forget, and it's time to remember.*

~ *What if you could live your life backward? Don't shrink back from those moments that invite you to reflect on the sunset of your life, for within them you will experience an awakening from the slumber of expectation, entitlement, and assumption.*

~ *Watch your inner dialogue and tone of voice with yourself and others.*

~ *Inner anxiety is caused when your body is where it is, and your mind is in the future or in the past. Be here now. When you release expectations and a desire for specific outcomes in order to feel accomplished, worthy, and enough, inner peace will return.*

~ *As Jesus' parable of the sower in Mark 4 says, be aware that worldly anxiety, the lure of riches, and material cravings all choke out your awareness of your God-given mission on Earth to grow in the ways of love. From these flow jealousy, comparison, envy, and selfish ambition, which block your ability to access your fullest God-given potential and life experience to create and inspire. Use the gifts with which you have been blessed for a greater good.*

~ *When you get out of your own way, the way of love floods in and all around you. Everything unfolds perfectly, like a beautiful rose, without any effort on your part. This is love's nature. Love evokes more love, and your joy is complete—heaven on Earth.*

~ *"Since we live by the Spirit let us keep in step with the Spirit. Let us not become conceited provoking and envying each other." (Galatians 5:26)*

~ *If you are not owned by your successes and failures, you are free "for a man is a slave to whatever has mastered him." (2 Peter 2:19). What has mastered you? The opinions and responses of those around you? Wake up from the drug of approval.*

~ *Do you rise and fall depending on the world's judgment? That gets old fast. It's time to adjust. God first, and then move out and light up the world.*

~ *"You O Lord keep my lamp burning; my God turns my darkness into light. With your help I can advance against a troop. With my God I can scale a wall." (Psalm 18:28–29)*

~ *Go for the soul feeling in life as if you are watching a sunrise or sunset. There is no need to control it. You are simply in the space of experiencing it. Step into the expansiveness of slow time when you give yourself permission to be present to the wonderment of life unfolding in front of your face.*

~ *Set the intention for each day by stating three things to which you are looking forward and three things for which you are grateful.*

Notes

Chapter 1

1. American Psychological Association, 2007 (*www.apa.org*).
2. Bob and Rachel Shaus, "Stress and Anxiety Symptoms," The American Institute of Stress, *http://proactivechange.com/stress/ statistics.htm*
3. Steven L. Sauter, *www.rethrival.net/stress-and-anxiety-symptoms.html*

Chapter 3

1. Bruce Lipton, *The Biology of Belief,* (Vista, CA: Hay House, Inc., 2011).
2. Dr. Richard A. DiCenso, "Behind The Curtain of The Unconscious—Energy Flows Where Attention Goes." *www.shapefit.com/behind-curtain-unconscious.html.*

Chapter 4

1. Anthony de Mello, *The Way to Love*. (New York: Image Books, Doubleday, 1995).

Chapter 6

1. *http://dictionary.reference.com/browse/hubris.*

Chapter 7

1. Joseph Esper, *Rules for the Discernment of Spirits*. (Manchester, N.H.: Sophia Institute Press, 2001).
2. Tony Stoltzfus, "NLP & Christian Coaching by Tony Husted," Christian Coaching Center, *www.christiancoachingcenter.org/index.php/2009/08/nlp-and-christian-coaching-by-tony-husted/* (accessed August 12, 2009).

Chapter 8

1. *http://ga.water.usgs.gov/edu/propertyyou.html.*
2. Masaru Emoto, *The Hidden Messages in Water*. (Hillsboro, OR.: Beyond Words Pub Co., 2004).
3. American University of NLP (*www.aunlp.org*). Reprinted with permission by Steve G. Jones.

Chapter 11

1. Susan Heitler, PhD, "Can Energy Therapies Really Help the PTSD from Senseless Killings?" *Resolution, Not Conflict*. October 13, 2011, *www.psychologytoday.com/blog/resolution-not-conflict/201110/energy-psychology-new-options-understanding-and-treating-emotion?-page=2.*

2. Steve Cole, MD, Erica Sloan, MD, and Patricia Ganz, MD, "Chronic Stress Accelerates Cancer Progression in Mice," *www.cancer.ucla.edu/index.aspx?recordid=397&page=644/.*

Chapter 12

1. Patricia Carrington, PhD, "Introducing the Choice Method." EFT Choice Method, Variations to Basic EFT. 2012. *www.masteringeft.com/Articles/EFTVariations/The_EFT_Choices_Method.htm*
2. Ibid.

Chapter 13

1. Gary Craig, founder of Emotional Freedom Technique (*www.Garythink.com*).
2. "Physical Exercise Can Prevent, Improve Cognitive Impairment." *http://newsblog.mayoclinic.org/2010/01/11/physical-exercise-can-prevent-improve-cognitive-impairment/*
3. Elizabeth Rice, "Physical Exercise Can Prevent, Improve Cognitive Impairment," *Archives of Neurology,* *http://newsblog.mayoclinic.org/2010/01/11/physical-exercise-can-prevent-improve-cognitive-impairment,* April 2012.
4. Angela Babb, "Walking and Other Exercise Help Prevent Dementia," *American Academy of Neurology, www.eurekalert.org/pub_releases/2007-12/aaon-wam121107.php*
5. Excerpted from my Master Certification Training. Reprinted with permission from Steve G. Jones, founder of the American University of NLP.
6. Ibid.

7. "Quick Coherence Technique," *www.heartmath.com/personal-use/quick-coherence-technique.html*

8. Gail Harris, "Lessons From the Heart," *Body & Soul with Gail Harris, www.pbs.org/bodyandsoul/203/heartmath.htm,* January 2011.

9. HeartMath "Quick Coherence Technique," *www.heartmath.com/personal-use/quick-coherence-technique.html,* January 2012.

10. Scott Miners, "Laughter Really Is the Best Medicine (Even If You Have to Fake It)," *Laughter Yoga International, www.laughteryoga.org/index.php?option=com_content&view=article&id=2225:laughter-really-is-the-best-medicine-even-if-you-have-to-fake-it&catid=237:news-archive&Itemid=480*

Chapter 14

1. Margerie Williams, *The Velveteen Rabbit.* (New York: George H. Doran Company, 1922).

Index

About the Author

Lauren E. Miller has received national recognition in *Redbook*, *Ladies Home Journal*, *Family Circle*, CNBC, MSN-BC, Lifetime, and Discovery, along with the *International Journal of Healing and Care*. With 10 years of proven experience and 18 years of intensive extended education in the areas of anxiety relief and stress reduction, Lauren works with men and women worldwide empowering them with techniques and skills to live life without stress using one-on-one coaching, teleseminars, seminars, and workshops. Lauren is a Certified Master NLP (Neuro Linguistic Programming) Practitioner and holds her Advanced Training Certificate in EFT (Emotional Freedom Technique), two energy psychology modalities that lead to profound inner transformation. As an international motivational speaker, Lauren has shared the stage with some of today's most inspirational speakers. She has survived two of life's top stressors at the same time: cancer and divorce. Her first book, *Hearing His Whisper*, is an Amazon Best Seller and Indie Book Award Winner. Her third book, *99 Things You Wish You Knew Before Stressing Out!*, is an award-winning international best-seller released in spring 2011. She is the founder of Stress Solutions University, an online stress relief video site equipping people with the mindset skills and physiological techniques needed to de-stress their lives quickly. As a VP for WhoZagood, a web 2.0 company, Lauren promotes ethical commerce between businesses and consumers. For more information please visit her Websites at:

www.laurenemiller.com
www.StressSolutionsUniversity.com
www.BeforeStressingOut.com

Continued Stress Relief Sources

We all know that stress is a silent killer. My name is Lauren E. Miller, and I personally understand the connection between stress and disease, as I was diagnosed with advanced breast cancer one week prior to my final divorce court date. Utilizing 20 years of training and teaching in the area of anxiety relief and stress management along with my personal experiences, I have created an online video/audio site equipping men and women with mindset skills and physiological techniques needed to make stress relief a life style: Stress Solutions University (SSU).

Stress Solutions University, SSU for short, is a community committed to providing easy to use resources that ignite and equip its members with specific stress relief mindset skills, perceptions, and quick tips that promote health, well-being, and personal excellence.

SSU utilizes the three main sensory acuity modalities: seeing, hearing, and feeling, to increase your ability to learn and apply the stress relief techniques, perceptions and skills:

99 Video Coaching Companion Series to my International best-selling book: *99 Things You Wish You Knew Before Stressing Out!* Containing one quick video stress relief tip per 99 things you wish you knew before stressing out…grab-go-stress relief.

Bi-Monthly Live Stress Relief Hotseat Coaching Calls (*replays made available to members*). Expanding each member's ability to de-stress now with quick tips and techniques addressing specific topics submitted by members. Support videos for the techniques are available.

Coaching with the Coaches: An ongoing series equipping members with quick stress relief techniques, perceptions, and tips from today's top thought leaders, coaches, and experts.

Instant Access to the e-book "*Release the Stress around Breast Cancer with Methods & Mantras for the Mastectomies of Life* (*www.breastcancerstressrelief.com*)

6 Step Signature Program for Busy Family Centered Women Entrepreneurs: Using NLP's 6 Logical Levels for personal excellence you will learn how to stay on track and achieve your goal in 30 days.

Check Out *www.StressSolutionsUniversity.com* and continue making stress relief a life style, bringing about a greater good in your life and the lives of those around you. Stress Solutions University.com makes life style stress solutions easy for you.